PENGUIN BOOKS — GREAT IDEAS

The Executioner

Joseph de Maistre
1753–1821

Joseph de Maistre

The Executioner

TRANSLATED BY RICHARD A. LEBRUN

PENGUIN BOOKS — GREAT IDEAS

PENGUIN BOOKS

Published by the Penguin Group
Penguin Books Ltd, 80 Strand, London WC2R 0RL, England
Penguin Group (USA) Inc., 375 Hudson Street, New York, New York 10014, USA
Penguin Group (Canada), 90 Eglinton Avenue East, Suite 700, Toronto, Ontario, Canada M4P 2Y3
(a division of Pearson Penguin Canada Inc.)
Penguin Ireland, 25 St Stephen's Green, Dublin 2, Ireland (a division of Penguin Books Ltd)
Penguin Group (Australia), 250 Camberwell Road, Camberwell, Victoria 3124, Australia
(a division of Pearson Australia Group Pty Ltd)
Penguin Books India Pvt Ltd, 11 Community Centre, Panchsheel Park, New Delhi – 110 017, India
Penguin Group (NZ), 67 Apollo Drive, Rosedale, North Shore 0632, New Zealand
(a division of Pearson New Zealand Ltd)
Penguin Books (South Africa) (Pty) Ltd, 24 Sturdee Avenue, Rosebank, Johannesburg 2196, South Africa

Penguin Books Ltd, Registered Offices: 80 Strand, London WC2R 0RL, England

www.penguin.com

Les soirées de Saint-Pétersbourg first published 1821
*St Petersburg Dialogues: Or Conversations on the Temporal Government of
Providence* translated and edited by Richard A. Lebrun first published in 1993

This selection first published in Penguin Books as *The Executioner* by kind permission of
McGill-Queen's University Press 2009

1

Copyright © McGill-Queen's University Press 1993

All rights reserved

Set by Rowland Phototypesetting Ltd, Bury St Edmunds, Suffolk
Printed in England by Clays Ltd, St Ives plc

Except in the United States of America, this book is sold subject
to the condition that it shall not, by way of trade or otherwise, be lent,
re-sold, hired out, or otherwise circulated without the publisher's
prior consent in any form of binding or cover other than that in
which it is published and without a similar condition including this
condition being imposed on the subsequent purchaser

978–0–141–19163–8

www.greenpenguin.co.uk

Penguin Books is committed to a sustainable future
for our business, our readers and our planet.
The book in your hands is made from paper
certified by the Forest Stewardship Council.

Contents

First Dialogue   1
Extracts from Second Dialogue   44
Seventh Dialogue   67

First Dialogue

At the end of a very warm day in the month of July 1809, I was returning up the Neva in a launch with Privy Councillor T***, a member of the Senate of St Petersburg, and Chevalier de B***, a young Frenchman who had been driven to this capital by the storms of the revolution in his country and by a series of bizarre events. Reciprocal esteem, a congruence of tastes, and some valuable relationships of service and hospitality had formed an intimate connection between us. Both of them were accompanying me that day to the country house where I was passing the summer. Although situated within the walls of the city, it was nevertheless far enough from the centre to be called *country* and to offer *solitude*; for much remains to be done before all the area within the city walls of St Petersburg is built up. Even though the open spaces to be found in the inhabited part are being filled in, it is still impossible to foresee whether the inhabitants will ever be able to advance to the limits traced by Peter the Great's bold finger.

It was a little after nine in the evening; the sun was setting, the weather superb. The soft breeze that was pushing us died in the sail we had seen *flapping*. The flag on the imperial palace, which announced the presence of the sovereign, soon fell limply along its supporting staff, heralding the stillness of the air. Our sailors took up their oars; we asked them to row slowly.

Nothing is rarer, nothing is more enchanting than a beautiful summer evening in St Petersburg. Whether the length of the winter and the rarity of these nights, which gives them a particular charm, renders them more desirable, or whether they really are so, as I believe, they are softer and calmer than evenings in more pleasant climates.

The sun, which in more temperate zones sinks quickly in the west leaving behind it only a brief twilight, here slowly brushes an earth it seems regretful to leave. Its disk surrounded with reddish haze rolls like a fiery chariot over the dark forests that crown the horizon, and its rays reflected in the windows of the palaces give the spectator the impression of a vast conflagration.

Great rivers usually have deep beds and steep banks that give them a wild appearance. The Neva flows full to its banks through the heart of a magnificent city. Its limpid waters skirt the grass of the islands it embraces, and through the entire extent of the city the river is contained by two granite embankments aligned as far as the eye can see, a kind of magnificence repeated along the three canals that go through the capital, and of which neither model nor imitation is to be found anywhere else.

A thousand boats cross and furrow the water in every direction. In the distance foreign vessels are furling their sails and dropping their anchors. They bring tropical fruit and the products of the whole world to this northern city. Brilliant American birds sail the Neva with orange groves; on arriving they find coconuts,

First Dialogue

pineapples, lemons, and all the fruits of their native land. Opulent Russians soon lay hands on the riches that have been presented to them, and, without counting, they throw their money to the avid merchants.

From time to time we meet elegant boats that have put up their oars and let themselves be carried quietly along the peaceful current of these beautiful waters. The rowers sing a folk song, while their masters enjoy in silence the beauty of the spectacle and the calm of the night.

Near us a small boat goes by rapidly with a wedding party of rich merchants. A crimson canopy decorated with a gold fringe covers a young couple and their parents. Squeezed between two lines of rowers a Russian band sends afar the sound of its noisy horns. This kind of music is peculiarly Russian and is perhaps the only thing particular to this people, whose culture is not old. Many people still alive know the inventor, whose name in this country constantly recalls the idea of old-fashioned hospitality, elegant luxury, and noble pleasures. Singular music! A ringing emblem fit to occupy the mind more than the ear. What does it matter to the piece that the instruments know what they are doing; twenty or thirty automatons acting together produce something alien to each. The individual is a blind mechanism; the ingenious calculation, the imposing harmony, is in the whole.

An equestrian statue of Peter I stands on the banks of the Neva at one end of the immense Isaac Square. His severe visage looks over the river and seems still to animate the navigation created by the genius of its founder. All that the ear can hear, all that the eye can see in this superb theatre, exists only because the thought of this powerful mind brought so many imposing monuments out of a swamp. Between these desolate rivers, where nature seemed to have exiled life, Peter placed his capital and created his subjects. His terrible arm is still extended over their posterity, who press around his august effigy. Looking at him, one does not know whether this bronze hand protects or threatens.

As our launch moves away, the song of the boatmen and the confused noise of the city fade away insensibly. The sun having descended below the horizon, the brilliant clouds shed a soft clarity, a golden half-light impossible to paint and that I have never seen elsewhere. The light and the shadows seem to mingle and conspire together to form a transparent veil covering the countryside.

If heaven in its goodness reserved for me one of those moments so rare in life where the heart is flooded with joy by some extraordinary and unexpected happiness, if a wife, children, and brothers separated from me for a long time without hope of reunion were suddenly to tumble into my arms, I would want it to happen here. Yes, I would want it to be on one of these beautiful nights on the banks of the Neva among these hospitable Russians.

Without openly sharing our feelings, we were enjoying the pleasures of the beautiful spectacle that surrounded us, when abruptly Chevalier de B*** broke the silence, exclaiming: 'I would like to have here in this boat with us one of those perverse men born for society's misfortune, one of those monsters that weary the earth . . .'

First Dialogue

And what would you do if he accommodated you? This was the question the two friends asked, speaking at the same time. 'I would ask him,' the Chevalier replied, 'if the night appeared as beautiful to him as it does to us.'

The Chevalier's exclamation pulled us out of our reverie. Soon his original idea engaged us in the following conversation, of which we were far from foreseeing the interesting consequences.

The Count

My dear Chevalier, perverse hearts never have beautiful nights or beautiful days. They can amuse themselves, or rather divert themselves, but they never know real enjoyment. I do not believe them capable of experiencing the same sensations that we experience. In any case, God keep them away from our boat.

The Chevalier

So you believe the wicked are not happy? I too would like to believe this; however every day I hear how they succeed in everything. If this were really the case, I would be a bit angry that Providence should have reserved the punishment of the wicked and the reward of the just entirely for the other world. It seems to me that a little on account for one and the other, even in this life, would not hurt anything. This is what makes me wish, as you have just seen, that the wicked were not susceptible to the sensations that delight us. I admit to you that I do not see this question very clearly. Surely you must tell me what you think, you, sirs, who are so learned in this kind of philosophy.

> As for me, raised in camps since in my childhood,
> I always leave the task of vengeance to heaven.

I admit to you again that I am not too well informed as to the way it pleases God to exercise his justice. To tell you the truth, though, it seems to me, on reflecting about what happens in the world, that if he punishes in this life, he at least does not press the matter.

The Count

Since you so desire, we might well devote the evening to the examination of this question, which is not so difficult in itself, but which has been muddled by the sophisms of Pride and her eldest daughter Irreligion. I greatly regret those *symposia*, of which antiquity has left us some valuable monuments. The ladies are undoubtedly lovable; we must live with them if we are not to become savages. Large gatherings have their place; it is even necessary to know how to participate in them with good grace. But when one has satisfied all the duties imposed by good manners, I find it very good that men sometimes assemble to reason, even at the table. I don't know why we do not imitate the ancients more on this

First Dialogue

point. Do you not think that the examination of an interesting question would occupy the after-dinner hour more usefully and more agreeably than the light or reprehensible conversations that animate ours? It seems to me it would be quite a good idea to sit Bacchus and Minerva down at the same table, one to defend the libertine, the other to be the pedant. We no longer have Bacchus; moreover our little *symposium* expressly rejects him. However we have a much better Minerva than the ancients; let us invite her to have tea with us. She is sociable and dislikes noise; I do hope she will come.

You already see before you, above the entrance of my house, a small terrace supported by four Chinese columns. My study opens directly onto that kind of belvedere, what you might call a large balcony. It is there, seated in an old armchair, that I peacefully await the arrival of sleep. Struck twice by lightning, as you know, I no longer have the right to what is vulgarly called *happiness*: I even confess to you it has too often happened that I have asked myself, *What is left for me?* But my conscience, forcing me to answer ME, made me blush at my weakness, and it's been a long time since I have even been tempted to complain. It is there in my observatory, especially, that I find delectable moments. Sometimes I surrender myself to sublime meditations and enter into a state that leads by degrees towards rapture. Sometimes, like an innocent magician, I evoke the venerable shades that once were for me terrestrial divinities and that today I evoke as tutelary geniuses. Often they seem to signal to me. But when I hurry towards them, charming memories remind me of what

I still have, and life appears to me as beautiful as if I were still in the age of hope.

When my oppressed heart demands repose, reading comes to my assistance. My books are all there under my hand: I require but few, for I have long been convinced of the perfect uselessness of very many works that still enjoy a great reputation . . .

The three friends having disembarked and taken their places around the tea table, the conversation resumed its course.

The Senator

I am delighted our Chevalier's sally made you think of the idea of a philosophical *symposium*. The subject we are going to treat could not be more interesting: *the happiness of the wicked and the misfortune of the just!* This is the great scandal to human reason. Could we employ an evening any better than in consecrating it to an examination of this mystery of divine metaphysics? We will be led to probe, at least as far as is permitted to human weakness, *the totality of the ways of Providence in the government of the moral world*. But I must warn you, Count, that it could well happen to you, as to the sultana *Scheherazade*, that you will not be able to quit after one evening. I am not saying that we will go on for a *thousand and one*; that would be an indiscretion. But at least we will meet more often than you imagine.

First Dialogue

The Count

I accept what you are telling me as a polite warning and not a threat. In any case, gentlemen, when you put questions to me, I can direct you to each other. I do not ask for or even accept the principal part in our conversations; if you are agreed, we will do our thinking in common. Only on that condition will I begin.

For a long time, gentlemen, there have been complaints against Providence in its distribution of good and evil. I must tell you that these difficulties have never been able to make the least impression on my mind. I see with the certitude of intuition, and I humbly thank Providence for this, that on this point man DECEIVES HIMSELF, in the full meaning of the phrase and in its natural sense.

I would like to be able to say like Montaigne: *man fools himself*; for this is exactly right. Yes, man no doubt *fools himself*; he is his own dupe. He takes the sophisms of his naturally rebellious heart (alas, nothing is more certain) for real doubts born in his understanding. If sometimes superstition *believes in belief*, as it has been reproached for doing, *pride believes in disbelief*. It is always man who *fools himself*, but the second case is much worse than the first.

Finally, gentlemen, there is no subject on which I feel more strongly than on the temporal government of Providence. So it is with complete conviction and lively satisfaction that I will disclose to two men whom I love tenderly some useful thoughts that I have collected along the already long route of a life entirely dedicated to serious studies.

The Chevalier

I will listen to you with the greatest pleasure, and I have no doubt that our common friend will accord you the same attention. But permit me, I beg you, to start by quibbling with you before you begin. And do not accuse me of *replying to your silence*, for it is as if you have already spoken and I know very well what you are going to tell me. You are, without the least doubt, on the point of beginning where preachers end, *with eternal life*. 'The wicked are happy in this world; but they will be chastised in the next; the just, on the other hand, suffer in this world, but will be happy in the next.' That is what we always hear. And why should I hide from you the fact that this trenchant reply does not satisfy me completely. I hope you will not suspect me of wishing to destroy or weaken this great proof, but it seems to me that it would not be harmed a bit by association with others.

The Senator

If the Chevalier is indiscreet or too precipitate, I confess that like him I have been wrong and just as wrong. For I was also on the point of quarrelling with you even before you had broached the question – or, if you wish me to speak more seriously, I would like to ask you to leave the beaten path. I have read many of your first-rate ascetic writers, whom I venerate immeasurably. However, even giving them all the praise they merit, I am pained to see that on this great question of the ways of divine justice in this world they almost all seem to accept criticisms of the fact, and to admit that there is no way of justifying divine Providence in this life. If this proposition is not false, it at least appears to me extremely dangerous. There is great danger in allowing men to believe that virtue will be recompensed and vice punished only in the other life. Unbelievers, for whom this world is everything, ask for nothing better, and the masses themselves necessarily follow the same line. Man is so distracted, so dependent on the objects that strike him, so dominated by his passions, that every day we see the most submissive believer risk the torments of the future life for the most wretched pleasure. What will happen to those who do not believe or whose belief is weak? So let us rely as much as you like on the future life, which responds to every objection. However, if a truly moral government exists in this world, and if, even in this life, crime must tremble, why relieve it of this fear?

The Count

Pascal observes somewhere that *the last thing that one discovers in writing a book is to know what to put at the beginning*. I am not writing a book, my friends, but I am beginning what will perhaps be a long discourse, and I would have had to think about where to begin. Happily, you have dispensed me from the labour of deliberation; you yourselves have shown me where I must start.

The familiar expression that one should address only to a child or to a subordinate, *You do not know what you are saying*, is nevertheless the comment that a sensible man has the right to make to the crowd that gets mixed up in discussing thorny questions of philosophy. Gentlemen, have you ever heard a soldier complain that in war musket balls hit only honest men, and that it suffices to be a scoundrel to be invulnerable? I am sure the answer is no, because in fact everyone knows that the balls make no distinction between persons. I would certainly have the right to establish at least a perfect equivalence between the evils of war in relation to soldiers and the evils of life in relation to all men. This equivalence, presumed to be exact, suffices by itself to eliminate a difficulty founded on a manifest falsehood. For it is not only false, but obviously FALSE *that it is generally the case that crime is happy and virtue unhappy in this world*. On the contrary, there is the greatest evidence that the distribution of blessings and misfortunes is a kind of lottery where each, without distinction, can draw a winning or a losing ticket. So we must change the question, and ask *why, in the temporal order, the just are not exempt from the evils that can afflict the guilty. We must ask why the wicked are not deprived of the good things that the just can enjoy*. But this question is altogether different from the first. I would even be quite astonished if its simple enunciation would not demonstrate its absurdity to you. It is one of my favourite ideas that the upright man is commonly enough warned by an interior feeling of the falsehood or truth of certain propositions before any analysis, often even without having the necessary studies to examine them with a complete knowledge of the case.

The Senator

I agree so strongly with you, and I like this doctrine so much, that I have perhaps exaggerated it by applying it to the natural sciences. Moreover I can, at least up to a certain point, invoke experience in this regard. More than once, with respect to physics or natural history, I have been shocked, without being able to say quite why, by certain accredited opinions. Then, afterwards, I have had the pleasure (for such it is) of seeing these opinions attacked and even ridiculed by men profoundly versed in these sciences, in which I am poorly versed as you know. Do you think that one need be the equal of Descartes to have the right to mock his vortices [*tourbillons*]? If someone comes to tell me that this planet on which we live is only a fragment of the sun torn off millions of years ago by a fantastic comet racing through space, or that animals are constructed like houses by putting this beside that, or that all the strata of our globe are only the fortuitous result of chemical precipitation, or a hundred other beautiful theories of this kind that have been produced in our century, is it necessary to have read a lot or to have reflected deeply, or to have been a member of four or five academies, to sense their absurdity? I go even farther. I believe that in those very questions that belong to the exact sciences, or which would appear to rest entirely on experiments, this rule of intellectual conscience is not entirely worthless for those not initiated in these kinds of knowledge. This is what has led me to doubt several things that usually pass for certain. I admit this to you in confidence. The explanation of tides by lunar and solar attraction, the decomposition and recomposition of water, and still other theories that I could cite for you and that are held as dogmas today, absolutely refuse to enter my mind. I feel myself inescapably led to believe that some honest scholar will come along someday to teach us that we were in error on certain of these great questions or that we did not understand them. Perhaps you will tell me (friendship has the right to do so) that *this is pure ignorance on my part*. I have said this to myself a thousand times. But tell me in your turn why I am not equally intractable to other truths. I believe them on the word of my teachers, and there has never arisen in my mind a single idea *against the faith*.

So where does this interior feeling come from, this feeling that revolts against certain theories? These theories are based on arguments that I do not know how to overturn, and yet this conscience we are discussing nevertheless tells us: *Quodcumque ostendis mihi sic, incredulus odi* ['Whatever you then show me, I discredit and abhor'. Horace].

First Dialogue

The Count

You are speaking Latin, Senator, although we are not living in a Latin country. It is all very well for you to make excursions to foreign lands; but according to the rules of etiquette you should have added, *with the permission of our Chevalier*.

The Chevalier

You are joking, Count. Please be aware that I am not as incompetent as you might think in the language of ancient Rome. It is true that I passed part of my youth in military camps, where Cicero is seldom cited, but I started out in a country where education itself usually began with Latin. I understand very well the passage that you have just cited, without however knowing where it comes from. In any case, I have no pretensions, on this point nor on so many others, to be the equal of the Senator, whose great and solid knowledge I honour most highly. He certainly has a right to say to me, even with a certain emphasis:

> . . . Go tell your fatherland,
> That there is *knowledge* on the borders of Scythia.

But please permit the youngest among you, gentlemen, to lead us back to the road from which we have strangely digressed. I do not know how we have drifted from Providence to Latin.

The Count

Whatever subject we treat, my dear friend, we are still talking about Providence. Moreover, a conversation is not a book; perhaps it is even better than a book precisely because it permits us to ramble a bit. However, let us return to our subject at the point where we left it. For the moment I will not examine to what degree we can rely on this interior feeling that the Senator so very justly calls *intellectual conscience*.

Even less will I permit myself to dispute the particular examples to which he has applied it; these details would carry us too far from our subject. I will say only that righteousness of heart and habitual purity of intention can have hidden influences and results that extend much farther than is commonly imagined. So I am very disposed to believe that among men such as those who now hear me, this secret instinct we have been talking about will often enough be right, even in the natural sciences. I am led to believe it nearly infallible in questions of rational philosophy, morality, metaphysics, and natural theology. It is infinitely worthy of the divine wisdom, which has created and regulated all things, to have dispensed man from science in everything that really matters to him. Therefore I was right to affirm that once the question occupying us was well posed, the interior agreement of every right-thinking mind would necessarily precede discussion.

The Chevalier

It seems to me that the Senator approves, since he does not object. As for me, I have always held to the maxim, *never contest useful opinions*. That the mind has a conscience like the heart, that an interior feeling leads man towards the good and puts him on guard against error, even in those things that seem to require preliminary preparation of study and reflection, is an opinion very worthy of divine wisdom and very honourable for man. Never to deny what is useful, never to support what can be harmful, this for me is a sacred rule that must always guide men like myself whose profession precludes profound studies. So do not expect any objection on my part. Nevertheless, without denying that my feelings have already taken sides, I would ask the Count to please address my reason.

The Count

I tell you again: I have never understood this eternal argument against Providence drawn from the misfortune of the just and the prosperity of the wicked. If the good man suffered because he is good and the wicked prospered precisely because he is wicked, the argument would be incontrovertible. It falls to the ground once one assumes that good and evil are distributed indifferently to all men. But false opinions resemble counterfeit money, which is struck by great scoundrels and then circulated by honest people who perpetuate the crime without knowing what they are doing. It was impiety that first made much ado with this objection, and though frivolity and flippancy have repeated it, there is, in truth, nothing to it. I come back to my first comparison: a good man is killed in war. Is this an injustice? No, it is a misfortune. If a man has gout or kidney stones, if his friend betrays him, if he is wiped out by the collapse of a building, etc., these again are misfortunes, but nothing more, since all men without distinction are subject to these sorts of accidents. Never lose sight of this great truth: *That a general law, if it is not unjust for all, cannot be so for the individual*. You do not have a particular illness, but you could have it; you have it, but you could have been exempt. The one who perished in a battle could have escaped; the one who returned could have fallen there. All are not dead, but all went there to die. So no more injustice: the just law is not that which affects everyone, but that which is made for everyone. The effect on such and such an individual is no more than an accident. To find difficulties in this order of things, we must love difficulties for their own sake. Unfortunately we do love them and look for them. The human heart, continually in revolt against the authority that constrains it, tells tales to the mind, which believes them. We accuse Providence to be dispensed from accusing ourselves. We raise against Providence difficulties that we would blush to raise against a sovereign or a simple administrator whose wisdom we can appreciate. How strange! It is easier for us to be just to men than to God.

It seems to me, gentlemen, that I would abuse your patience if I went any further in proving to you that the question is usually poorly posed. They really *do not know what they are saying* when they complain that vice is happy and virtue unhappy in this world. Even on the supposition most favourable to the grumblers, it is manifestly proved that evils of all kinds fall on the human race, like musket balls on an army, with no distinction of persons. Moreover, if the good man does not suffer *because he is good*, and if the wicked man does not prosper *because he is wicked*, the objection disappears, and good sense has triumphed.

The Chevalier

I admit that if only the distribution of physical or external misfortunes is considered, there is evidently inattention or bad faith in the objection against Providence drawn from this argument. But it seems to me that it is the impunity of crimes that is more insisted upon. This is the great scandal, and this is the issue about which I am most curious to hear what you have to say.

Joseph de Maistre

The Count

My friend, it is not yet time. You have let me win a little too quickly with respect to the evils that you call *external*. If I have always supposed, as you have seen, that these evils are equally distributed among all men, I have done so only for the sake of argument, for in truth this is not the case. But before going any further, let us take heed, if you please, not to leave our route. There are questions that touch each other, so to speak, so that it is easy to slip from one to another without noticing it. So, for example, the question *Why do the just suffer?*, leads imperceptibly to another: *Why do men suffer?* The second however is quite a different question; it is that of the origin of evil. Let us therefore begin by avoiding all equivocation. *Evil is on the earth*; alas, this is a truth that need not be proved. But there is more: *it is there very justly, and God could not have been its author*. This is another truth that I hope neither of us doubt, and that I can dispense myself from proving, since I know to whom I am speaking.

The Senator

I profess this very truth with all my heart and without any qualification; but this profession of faith, precisely because of its latitude, requires an explanation. Your St Thomas said with the logical laconism that distinguished him: *God is the author of evil that punishes, but not of the evil that defiles*. He is certainly right in one sense; but it is necessary to understand him correctly. God is the author of the evil *that punishes*, that is to say physical evil or suffering, as the sovereign is the author of the punishments that are inflicted by his laws. In a remote sense, it is certainly the sovereign himself who hangs men and breaks them on the wheel, since all authority and every legal execution derive from him. But in the direct or immediate sense, it is the thief, it is the forger, it is the assassin, etc., who are the real authors of the *evils that punish them*. They are the ones who build the prisons, who erect the gallows and the scaffolds. In all this the sovereign acts like Homer's Juno, *with his own will, yet with soul unwilling*.

It is the same with God (always excluding any rigorous comparison, which would be insolent). Not only can he not be, in any sense, the author of moral evil, or *sin*, but he cannot even be understood to be the original author of physical evil, which would not exist if intelligent creatures had not rendered it necessary by abusing their freedom. Plato said it, and nothing is more obvious in itself: *the good being cannot wish to harm anyone*. But since we would never maintain that a good man ceased to be such because he justly chastised his son, or because he killed an enemy on the battlefield, or because he sent a scoundrel to punishment, let us take care, as you said a little while ago, Count, not to be less equitable towards God than towards men. Every right-thinking mind is convinced by intuition that evil cannot come from an all-powerful being. It was this infallible feeling that formerly taught Roman good sense to unite as if by a necessary bond the two august titles of MOST GOOD and MOST POWERFUL. This magnificent expression, though born under the sign of paganism, appeared so just that it has passed into your religious language, so delicate and so exclusive. I will even tell you in passing that it has occurred to me more than once to think that the antique inscription, IOVI OPTIMO MAXIMO, could be put in full on the pediments of your Latin temples, for what is IOV-I if not IOV-AH? [Jupiter if not Jehovah].

The Count

You know very well that I do not wish to dispute anything you have just said. Undoubtedly *physical evil could only have come into the world through the fault of free creatures. It can only be there as a remedy or an expiation, and in consequence it cannot have God as its direct author.* For us these are incontestable dogmas. Now I come back to you, Chevalier. You admitted just now that one can scarcely quibble with Providence over the distribution of good and evil, but that the scandal lies above all in the impunity of scoundrels. I doubt, however, if you could renounce the first objection without abandoning the second. If there is no injustice in the distribution of ills, on what will you base the complaints of virtue? The world is governed by general laws. So if the foundations of the terrace on which we are speaking were suddenly thrown into the air by some subterranean disturbance, I do not believe that you would claim that God would be obliged to suspend the laws of gravity in our favour

First Dialogue

because at the moment this terrace holds three men who have never murdered or stolen. We would certainly fall and be crushed. The same would happen if we had been members of the Illuminati lodge of Bavaria or of the Committee of Public Safety. Would you want things arranged so that when it hails the fields of the just man are spared? That would be a miracle. But if, by chance, this just man were to commit a crime after the harvest, then it would have to rot in his granary. That would be another miracle. Each moment would require another miracle, and miracles would become the ordinary state of the world. This is to say that there would no longer be any miracles, since exceptions would become the rule, and disorder order. To set forth such ideas is to refute them sufficiently.

What still deceives us often enough on this point is that, without our perceiving it, we cannot prevent ourselves from ascribing to God our own ideas about the dignity and importance of persons. In relation to ourselves these ideas are quite just, since we are all subject to the order established in society. But when we carry them into the general order, we resemble the queen who said: *When it is a question of damning people like us, you can well believe that God will think more than once.* Elizabeth of France mounted the scaffold; Robespierre followed a bit later. By coming into the world, the angel and the monster both subjected themselves to all the general laws that rule here. No words can describe the crime of these scoundrels who caused the purest and most august blood in the world to flow. Yet in relation to the general order, there is no injustice; this is still a misfortune attached to the human condition, and nothing more. *Every man as man is subject to all the misfortunes of humanity*: the law is general, so it is not unjust. To claim that a man's rank or virtues should exempt him from the action of an iniquitous or misguided tribunal, is precisely the same as wanting such honours to exempt him from apoplexy, for example, or even death.

Observe, however, that, in spite of these general and necessary laws, this supposed equality, on which I have insisted up to now, is far from being the actual case. I have assumed it, as I have told you, *for the sake of my argument*; but nothing is more false, as you will see.

First, let us begin by taking no account of the individual. The general law, the visible and visibly just law, is *that the greatest amount of happiness, even temporal, belongs, not to the virtuous man, but to virtue*. If it were to be otherwise, there would no longer be vice, nor virtue, nor merit, nor demerit, and in consequence, no more moral order. Suppose that each moral action were *paid*, so to speak, by some temporal advantage; the act, having nothing more of the supernatural, would no longer merit a recompense of this kind. Suppose, on the other hand, that in virtue of some divine law the thief's hand should fall off the moment he committed a theft. People would refrain from theft as they refrain from putting their hands under the butcher's cleaver. The moral order would disappear entirely. Therefore to reconcile this order (the sole order possible for intelligent beings, and that which is, moreover, proved by the facts) with the laws of justice, it is necessary that virtue be recompensed and vice punished, even in this world – but not always, nor immediately. It is necessary that the incomparably greater portion of temporal happiness be attributed to virtue, and the proportional amount of unhappiness fall to vice, but that the individual never be sure of anything. In fact, this is the case. Imagine any other hypothesis; it will lead you directly to the destruction of the moral order, or to the creation of another world.

To come now to particulars, let us begin, please, with human justice. God, wanting to govern men by men, at least exteriorly, has handed over to sovereigns the eminent prerogative of punishing crimes, and it is in this matter especially that they are his representatives. I found an admirable piece on this subject in the laws of Manu. Permit me to read it to you from the third volume of *The Works of Sir William Jones*, which is there on my table.

The Chevalier

Read if you wish; but after having the goodness to tell me about this king Manu, for I have never heard of him.

The Count

Manu, Chevalier, was the great legislator of India. Some say he was the son of the Sun, others that he was the son of Brahma, the first person of the Indian trinity. Between these two opinions, equally probable, I remain suspended without hope of deciding. Unfortunately, it is equally impossible for me to tell you in what period one or the other of these two fathers might have engendered Manu. Sir William Jones, of learned memory, believed that this legislator's code was perhaps anterior to the Pentateuch, and *certainly* at the very least anterior to all the lawgivers of Greece. But Mr Pinkerton, who also has a good claim on our confidence, has taken the liberty of mocking the brahmins. He believes himself able to prove that Manu could well have been an honest jurist of the thirteenth century. My custom is not to dispute such slight differences. So, gentlemen, I am going to read to you the piece in question, whose date we are going to leave blank. Listen well.

'For his use Brahma formed in the beginning of time the genius of punishment, with a body of pure light, his own son, even abstract criminal justice, the protector of all created things. Through fear of that genius, all sentient beings, whether fixed or locomotive, are fitted for natural enjoyments and swerve not from duty. When the king, therefore, has fully considered place and time, and his own strength, and the divine ordinance, let him justly inflict punishment on all those who act unjustly. Punishment is an active ruler; he is the true manager of public affairs; he is the dispenser of laws; and wise men call him the *sponsor* of all the four orders for the discharge of their several duties. Punishment governs all mankind; punishment alone preserves them; punishment wakes, while their guards are asleep; the wise consider punishment as the perfection of justice. If the king were not, without indolence, to punish the guilty, the stronger would roast the weaker. The whole race of men is kept in order by punishment; for a guiltless man is hard to find: through fear of punishment, indeed, this universe is enabled to enjoy its blessings. All classes would become corrupt; all barriers would be destroyed; there would be total confusion among men, if punishment either were not inflicted, or were inflicted unduly. But where punishment, with a black hue and a red eye, advances to destroy sin, there if the judge discern well, the people are undisturbed.'

The Senator

Admirable! Magnificent! You are an excellent man for having unearthed for us this piece of Indian philosophy. In truth, the date does not matter.

The Count

It made the same impression on me. I find there European reason with a just measure of that Oriental emphasis that pleases everyone when it is not exaggerated. I do not believe it possible to express with more nobility and energy this divine and terrible prerogative of sovereigns: *the punishment of the guilty*.

But having forewarned you with these sombre thoughts, allow me to direct your attention for a moment to a subject that is undoubtedly shocking. It is nevertheless very worthy of occupying our reflections.

This formidable prerogative of which I have just

spoken results in the necessary existence of a man destined to administer the punishments adjudged for crimes by human justice. This man is, in effect, found everywhere, without there being any means of explaining how; for reason cannot discover in human nature any motive capable of explaining this choice of profession. I believe you too accustomed to reflection, gentlemen, not to have thought often about the executioner. So who is this inexplicable being who, when there are so many pleasant, lucrative, honest, and even honourable professions in which he could exercise his strength or dexterity to choose among, has chosen that of torturing and putting to death his own kind? Are this head and this heart made like our own? Do they contain anything that is peculiar and alien to our nature? For myself, I have no doubt about this. In outward appearance he is made like us; he is born like us. But he is an extraordinary being, and for him to be brought into existence as a member of the human family a particular decree was required, a FIAT of creative power. He is created as a law on to himself.

Consider how he is viewed by public opinion, and try to conceive, if you can, how he could ignore this opinion or confront it! Scarcely have the authorities assigned his dwelling, scarcely has he taken possession of it, when other men move their houses elsewhere so they no longer have to see his. In the midst of this seclusion and in this kind of vacuum formed around him, he lives alone with his female and his offspring, who acquaint him with the human voice. Without them he would hear nothing but groans . . . A dismal signal is given. An

First Dialogue

abject minister of justice knocks on his door to warn him that he is needed. He sets out. He arrives at a public square packed with a pressing and panting crowd. He is thrown a poisoner, a parricide, a blasphemer. He seizes him, stretches him out, ties him to a horizontal cross, and raises his arms. Then there is a horrible silence; there is no sound but the crack of bones breaking under the crossbar and the howls of the victim. He unties him and carries him to a wheel. The broken limbs are bound to the spokes, the head hangs down, the hair stands on end, and the mouth, gaping like a furnace, occasionally emits a few bloody words begging for death. He has finished; his heart is pounding, but it is with joy. He congratulates himself. He says in his heart, *No one can break men on the wheel better than I*. He steps down; he holds out his blood-stained hand, and justice throws him from afar a few gold coins, which he carries away through a double row of men drawing back in horror. He sits down to table and eats; then he goes to bed and sleeps. Awakening on the morrow, he thinks of something quite different from what he did the day before. Is this a man? Yes. God receives him in his shrines and allows him to pray. He is not a criminal, and yet no tongue would consent to say, for example, *that he is virtuous, that he is an honest man, that he is admirable*, etc. No moral praise seems appropriate for him, since this supposes relationships with human beings, and he has none.

And yet all greatness, all power, all subordination rests on the executioner; he is both the horror and the bond of human association. Remove this incomprehensible agent from the world, and in a moment order gives way to chaos, thrones fall, and society disappears. God, who is the author of sovereignty, is therefore also the author of punishment. He has suspended our earth on these two poles; *For the pillars of the earth are the Lord's, and he has set the world upon them.*

There is then in the temporal sphere a divine and visible law for the punishment of crime. This law, as stable as the society it upholds, has been executed invariably since the beginning of time. Evil exists on the earth and acts constantly, and by a necessary consequence it must constantly be repressed by punishment. All over the globe what we see is the constant action of all governments stopping or punishing criminal outrages. The sword of justice has no sheath; it must always be threatening or striking. For whom are there knouts, gallows, wheels, and stakes? For criminals, obviously. Judicial errors are exceptions that do not upset the rule; moreover I have a number of reflections to propose to you on this point. In the first place, these fatal errors are far less frequent than is imagined. Public opinion is always opposed to authority whenever there is the least room for doubt. So it avidly welcomes the least rumours of purported judicial murder. A thousand individual passions can add to this general trend. But from long experience I swear to you, Senator, that it is an excessively rare thing for a court to put someone to death through passion or error. You are laughing, Chevalier!

First Dialogue

The Chevalier

I was just thinking of the *Calas family*; and the Calas made me think *of the horse and the whole stable*.* That is how ideas are connected and how the imagination is always interrupting reason.

The Count

Do not apologize, for you have been of service to me in making me think of this famous decision, which furnishes me with another proof of what I have just been telling you. Nothing is less well proved, gentlemen, than the innocence of Calas. There are a thousand reasons to doubt it, and even to believe the contrary. But nothing struck me more than an original letter from Voltaire to the celebrated Tronchin of Geneva, a letter I was able to read some years ago. In the midst of a very animated public discussion, where Voltaire is showing off and giving himself the title of the tutor of innocence and avenger of humanity, he clowns as if he were speaking about comic opera. I especially recall this phrase, which struck me: *You were right in finding my memoir too heated,*

---

* [At the time when the memory of the falsely executed Calas was being rehabilitated, Duke d' A. . . . asked a resident of Toulouse *how it could happen that one of their courts had been so cruelly deceived*; to which the second replied by citing the common proverb: *There is no good horse who has never shied*. To which the Duke quickly responded, *but a whole stable!*]

but I am preparing another for you in a hotter bath [au bain marie]. It is in this grave and sentimental style that this worthy man was speaking in the ear of his confidant at the same time Europe was resounding to his fanatical *Lamentations*.

But let Calas be. That an innocent perishes is a misfortune like any other. That a guilty man escapes is another exception of the same kind. But it always remains true, generally speaking, *that there is on the earth a universal and visible order for the temporal punishment of crimes*. I must also have you notice that the guilty do not deceive the eye of justice as often as one might suppose given the infinite precautions they take to hide themselves. In the circumstances that unmask the most cunning scoundrels there are often things so unexpected, so surprising, so *unpredictable*, that men who are led by their profession or by their reflections to follow affairs of this sort find themselves inclined to believe that human justice is not left entirely denuded of a certain extraordinary assistance in seeking out the guilty.

Allow me to add another consideration to conclude this chapter on punishments. Just as it is possible that we are in error when we accuse human justice of sparing a guilty man, because the one we regard as such is not really guilty, on the other side, it is equally possible that a man tortured for a crime he did not commit really merited punishment for an absolutely unknown crime. Happily and unfortunately, there are several examples of this kind proved by the confession of criminals. And there are, I believe, an even greater number of which we are ignorant. This last supposition merits especially close

First Dialogue

attention. Although in this case the judges are extremely blameworthy or unfortunate, Providence, for whom all things, even obstacles, are means, is no less served by crime or ignorance in executing the temporal justice that we demand. It is sure that these two suppositions notably restrain the number of exceptions. So you see how this assumed equality, which I first supposed, is already disrupted by the consideration of human justice alone.

Turning from the corporal punishments inflicted by justice, let us consider illnesses. You have already anticipated me. If every kind of intemperance were removed from the world, most maladies would be driven out as well, and it is even possible that we could say that all of them would disappear. This is something that everyone can see in a general and confused way, but it is good to examine the matter more closely. If there were no moral evil on the earth, there would be no physical illness. And since an infinity of illnesses is the immediate product of certain moral disorders, is it not true that the analogy would lead us to generalize the observation? Have you by chance read Seneca's vigorous and sometimes a bit distasteful tirade on the illnesses of his time? It is interesting to see that Nero's time was marked by a deluge of diseases unknown to the preceding period. Seneca exclaims agreeably: 'Are you astonished by this innumerable quantity of illnesses? Count the cooks.' He is especially angry with the women: 'Hippocrates, the illustrious founder of the guild and profession of medicine, remarked that women never lost their hair or suffered from pain in their feet; and yet nowadays they run short of hair and are afflicted with gout. They have put off their womanly nature and are therefore condemned to suffer the diseases of men. *May heaven curse them for the infamous usurpation that these miserable creatures have dared to perpetrate on our sex!*' Undoubtedly there are illnesses that are only the accidental results of a general law, as will never be said often enough: the most moral man must die. Of two men who run a forced race, the one to save his fellow man, the other to assassinate him, one or the other can die of pleurisy. But what a frightening number of illness in general and accidents in particular are due only to our vices. I recall that Bossuet, preaching before Louis XIV and his whole court, called on medicine to testify to the deadly consequences of sensual pleasure. He was largely correct to cite what is most obvious and most striking, but it would have been right to generalize the observation. For my part, I cannot disagree with the opinion of a recent apologist who held that all illnesses have their origin in some vice proscribed by Scripture, and that this holy law contains true medicine for the body as well as the soul, so that if a society of just men made use of it, death would be no more than the inevitable term of a sane and robust old age. This opinion was, I believe, that of Origen. What deceives us on this point is that when the effect is not immediate we no longer perceive it; but it is no less real. Sicknesses, once established, propagate themselves, grow, and amalgamate with deadly affinity, so that we can suffer today the physical penalty of an excess committed a century ago. However, despite the confusion resulting from these horrible mixtures, the comparison between crimes and illnesses is plain to every attentive observer. As with sins,

First Dialogue

there are illnesses that are *actual and original, accidental and habitual, mortal and venial*. There are diseases of laziness, of anger, of gluttony, of incontinence, etc. Moreover observe that there are crimes that have distinctive characteristics, and consequently distinctive names in every language, such as murder, sacrilege, incest, etc., and others that can only be identified by general terms, such as fraud, injustice, violence, corruption, etc. In the same way there are distinctive diseases such as dropsy, consumption, and apoplexy, etc., and others that can only be identified by the general terms of malaise, discomfort, aches, and *nameless* fevers, etc. Now the more virtuous the man, the more immune he is from illnesses *that have names*.

Bacon, although a Protestant, as a good observer could not help noticing the great number of saints (monks especially and hermits) whom God had favoured with a long life, nor help making the contrary no less striking observation that there is not a vice, not a crime, not a disordered passion that does not produce in the physical order a more or less fatal, more or less long term, effect. A beautiful analogy between illnesses and crimes can be drawn from the action of the divine author of our religion. Since he was the master certainly, he could have confirmed his mission in men's eyes by enkindling volcanoes or bringing down lightning, but he never derogated from the laws of nature except to do good things for men. Before healing the sick who were presented to him, this divine master never failed to remit their sins or to render public testimony to the faith that had reconciled the sinner. What is even more striking is what he said to the lepers: 'You see that I have healed you; take care now to sin no more, for fear that something worse happens to you.'

It even seems that we are somehow led to penetrate to a great secret if we reflect on a truth whose very enunciation is a demonstration for any man who knows something of philosophy: we can know 'that no illness is known to have a physical cause.' However, although reason, revelation, and experience unite to convince us of the deadly connection that exists between moral evil and physical evil, not only do we refuse to perceive the material consequences of those passions that reside only in the soul, but we do not examine enough or closely enough those that have their roots in physical organs or whose visible consequences must frighten us even more. For example, we have repeated a thousand times the old adage, *that the table kills more men than war*, but there are very few men who reflect enough on the deep truth of this axiom. If everyone examines themselves severely, they will remain convinced that they eat perhaps half again more than they should. For excesses of quantity let us pass to excesses of quality. Examine in all its details this perfidious art of exciting a deceptive appetite that kills us. Think of all the innumerable caprices of intemperance, of those seductive *compositions* that are to our body precisely what bad books are to our mind, which is at the same time overloaded and corrupted. You will see clearly how nature, continually attacked by these vile excesses, struggles vainly against our endless attacks. You will see how the body must, despite its marvellous resources, finally succumb, and how it accepts the germs

First Dialogue

of a thousand illnesses. Philosophy alone discovered long ago that all human wisdom is to be found in two words: SUSTINE ET ABSTINE [suffer and abstain]. And although philosophy is a feeble legislator whose best laws may even be ridiculed because it lacks the power to make itself obeyed, nevertheless we must be fair and give it credit for the truths that it has published. It has understood very well that man's strongest inclinations are vicious to the point of obviously tending towards the destruction of society, that man has no greater enemy than himself, and that when he has learned to vanquish himself, he knows everything. But the Christian law, which is nothing but the revealed will of him who knows everything and can do everything, does not limit itself to vain counsels. It has made of abstinence, of habitual victory over our desires, a capital precept that must regulate man's entire life. Moreover, it has made the more or less severe, more or less frequent, privation of the permitted pleasures of the table a fundamental law that can be modified according to the circumstances, but that always remains invariable in its essence. If we would like to think about this privation called *fasting*, considering it from a spiritual point of view, it suffices for us to discover and understand the Church when she says to God, with an infallibility that she has received from him: *You use bodily fasting to raise our spirits to you, to repress our vices, and to give us virtues you can reward*. But I do not want to leave the temporal sphere just yet. Often I think with admiration and even gratitude of this salutary law that opposes legal and periodic abstinences to the destructive action that intemperance continually exercises on our organs, and that at least prevents this force from accelerating by obliging it to keep beginning anew. Nothing wiser can be imagined, even under the heading of simple hygiene; never has there been better agreement between man's temporal advantage and his interests and needs of a superior order.

The Senator

You have just indicated one of the great sources of physical evil, which alone justifies in great part the ways of Providence in its temporal governance, when we dare judge it in this way. But the most unrestrained passion and the one that is the dearest to human nature is also one that must attract our attention, since from it alone flows more temporal evils than all the other vices together. We have a horror of murder. But what are all murders put together, or war even, compared to the vice that is like the evil principle, *murderer from the beginning*, that acts on potential life, that kills what does not yet exist, and that does not cease to stop up the very sources of life by weakening them and defiling them? Since there is in the world in its present state an immense conspiracy to justify, to embellish, and – I almost said – to consecrate this vice, there is no other vice on which the pages of Scripture have accumulated more temporal anathemas. The sage denounces for us with redoubled wisdom the deadly consequences of these *guilty nights*. If we look around us with pure and well-directed eyes, nothing can prevent us from observing the incontestable

First Dialogue

accomplishment of these anathemas. Human reproduction, which from one point of view approaches that of brutes, is from another point of view elevated as high as pure intelligence by the law that surrounds this great mystery of nature, and by the sublime participation accorded to those who make themselves worthy of it. But these laws have a terrible sanction! If we could clearly perceive all the evils that result from disordered procreation and from innumerable profanations of the first law of the world, we would recoil in horror. This is why the only true religion is also the only one that, without the power to say all things to man, nevertheless lays hold of marriage and submits it to its holy ordinances. I even believe that its legislation on this question must be placed high among the most tangible proofs of its divinity. The sages of antiquity, although denied the revelation that we possess, were nevertheless nearer to the origin of things and some remnants of primitive traditions had come down to them. We see that they were very much occupied with this important subject, for not only did they believe that moral and physical vices were transmitted from fathers to their children, but by a natural consequence of this belief they warned men to examine carefully the state of their souls when they seemed to be obeying only material laws. What would they not have said if they had known what man has become and what he can desire! So men have brought upon themselves most of the evils that afflict them; they suffer justly what they make others suffer in turn. Our children will carry the penalty of our faults; our fathers are avenged in them in advance.

Joseph de Maistre

The Chevalier

You know very well, my respectable friend, that if you were heard by certain men of my acquaintance, they could very well accuse you of being an illuminist.

The Senator

If these men of whom you speak were to address this compliment (literally) to me, I would thank them sincerely, since there would be nothing more honourable than to really be *illuminated*. But that is not what you intended. In any case, if I am an *illuminist*, at least I am not one of those of whom we were speaking earlier. My *enlightenment* surely does not come from them. For the rest, if the nature of our studies sometimes leads us to thumb through the works of some extraordinary men, you yourself have furnished me with a sure rule to keep us from being led astray, a rule to which you constantly submit your conduct, as you told us just a moment ago. This rule is one of general utility. When an opinion shocks no known truth, and when moreover it tends to elevate man, to perfect him, to make him master of his passions, I do not see why we would reject it. Can man be too convinced of his spiritual dignity? He would certainly not be deceiving himself in believing that it is of the highest importance for him never to act like a blind instrument of Providence in those things that are given over to his power, but to act like an intelligent, free, and obedient minister, with the anterior and determined will to obey the plans of the one who sent him. If he is mistaken on the extent of the effects he attributes to his own will, it must be admitted that he is innocently mistaken, and I dare add quite happily mistaken.

The Count

With all my heart I accept this rule of utility, which is common to all men; but we have another, you and I, Chevalier, which protects us from all error – it is that of authority. They can say or write what they wish; our fathers have thrown out an anchor, and holding on to it, we no more fear the illuminists than the impious. So leaving aside from this discussion everything that could be seen as hypothetical, I am still entitled to pose this incontestable principle: *Moral vices can augment the number and intensity of diseases to a degree that is impossible to determine. Reciprocally, this hideous empire of physical evil can be restrained by virtue to limits that are also impossible to fix.* As there is not the least doubt on the truth of this proposition, there is no need to go further to justify the ways of Providence in the temporal order, especially if one adds to this consideration that of human justice, since it has been demonstrated that from this double point of view the privileges of virtue are incalculable, independently of any appeal to reason and even of any religious consideration. Would you now like to leave the temporal order?

The Chevalier

I am beginning to get a little bored by all these earthly considerations, so I would not be upset if you had the goodness to transport me to something a little higher. So therefore . . .

The Senator

I am opposed to that voyage this evening. The pleasure of our conversation has seduced us and the length of the day has deceived us, for the clock has just sounded midnight. So with faith in our watches, let us go to bed, and tomorrow we will be faithful to our appointment.

The Count

You are right. Men of our age, in this season, must prescribe for themselves a conventional night of peaceful sleep, just as in winter they must create an artificial day for themselves for the sake of work. As for our Chevalier, nothing prevents him from amusing himself in fashionable society after quitting his grave friends. Undoubtedly he will find more than one house where they are still at table.

First Dialogue

The Chevalier

I will profit from your counsel, on the condition however that you will do me the favour of believing that I am not sure, with great differences, of amusing myself *in fashionable society* as much as here. But tell me, before we part, if good and evil are not, by chance, distributed in the world like day and night. Today we light candles only for form; in six months we will scarcely extinguish them. In Quito [at the Equator] they light them and extinguish them at the same hour every day. Between these two extremes, day and night lengthen from the equator to the pole, and in a contrary sense in invariable order. But at the end of the year, each has his own account, and each man has received his four thousand three hundred and eighty hours of day and as much of night. Count, what do you think of this?

The Count

We will talk about it tomorrow.

Extracts from *Second Dialogue*

The Count

You are turning your cup over, Chevalier. Don't you want any more tea?

The Chevalier

No, thank you. This evening I will take only one cup. Raised in a southern province of France, as you know, where tea was drunk only as a cold remedy, I have since lived among people who use this beverage habitually So I take it to do like the others, but without ever finding it pleasurable enough to find I need it. On principle, moreover, I am not a great partisan of new drinks; who knows if they may not bring us new illnesses.

The Senator

That could well be, although without increasing the total of diseases in the world, for in supposing that the cause you have indicated has produced some new illnesses or discomforts, which would seem to me difficult to prove, one would also have to take account of diseases that have been considerably weakened or even almost totally disappeared, such as leprosy, elephantiasis, and gangrene. In any case, nothing leads me to think that tea, coffee, and sugar, which have become so prodigiously popular in Europe, were given to us as punishments; I am rather inclined to see them as gifts. But one way or the other, I will never regard them as indifferent. Nothing happens by chance in the world, and I have long suspected that the exchange of food and beverages among men belongs in some way to a secret purpose operating in the world without our knowledge. For every man with a keen eye who wants to see, there is nothing so apparent as the link between the two worlds; or to put it better, there is only one world, rigorously speaking, since matter is nothing. Try, if you will, to imagine matter existing alone without intelligence you will never be able to do it.

The Count

I also think that no one can deny the relationship between the visible and invisible worlds. The denials come from a double way of looking at the two worlds, for one or the other can be considered, or one in itself or in its relation to the other. It was in following this natural division that I first examined the question that occupies us. I considered only the temporal order, and I had just asked your permission to ascend higher when I was very appropriately interrupted by the Senator. Today I will continue.

Since every evil is a punishment, it follows that no evil should be considered necessary; and since no evil is necessary, it follows that all evil can be prevented, either by suppression of the crime that made it necessary, or by prayer, which has the power of preventing or mitigating it. The empire of physical evil can therefore be restrained indefinitely by this supernatural means, as you see . . .

The Chevalier

Allow me to interrupt you and even to be a little impolite, if necessary, to force you to be clearer. You are touching here on a subject that has more than once disturbed me deeply; but for the moment I will defer my questions on this point. I should just like to point out to you that, unless I am mistaken, you are confusing the evils directly due to the faults of those who suffer them with those that are transmitted to us by an unfortunate heritage. You said *that we perhaps suffer today from excesses committed more than a century ago*; now it seems to me that we should not have to answer for these crimes as well as for that of our first parents. I do not believe that faith extends as far as that; and, if I am not mistaken, original sin is quite enough, since this sin alone has subjected us to all the miseries of this life. So it seems to me that the physical evils that come to us by inheritance have nothing in common with the temporal government of Providence.

Extracts from *Second Dialogue*

The Count

Please note, I ask you, that I did not insist on this sad heredity, and that I did not cite it as a direct proof of the justice Providence exercises in this world. I spoke of it in passing as of an observation found along my way; but I thank you with all my heart, my dear Chevalier, for having brought it back to our attention, since it is well worth our consideration. If I have not made any distinction between illnesses, it is because they are all punishments. Original sin, which explains everything and without which nothing is explained, unfortunately repeats itself at every moment in time, although in a secondary way. I do not believe that this idea, when it is developed accurately for you, contains anything shocking to your intelligence as a Christian. Original sin is undoubtedly a mystery; however, if a man examines it closely he finds that this mystery, like others, has its plausible sides, even for our limited intelligence.

Let us leave to one side for the moment the theological question of *imputation*, which remains intact, and limit ourselves to the common observation, which accords so well with our most natural ideas, *that all beings with the faculty of reproduction will produce beings similar to themselves*. The rule suffers no exception; it is written everywhere in the universe. If such a being is degraded, its offspring will never resemble that being's primitive condition, but the state to which it has declined through some cause. This is very plain, and the rule holds in the physical as well as in the moral order. But it must be noted that there is the same difference between a *crippled man* and a *sick man* as there is between a *vicious* man and a *guilty* man. Acute illness is not transmissible, but that which vitiates the humours becomes an *original illness* capable of tainting a whole race.

It is the same with moral illnesses. Some belong to the ordinary state of human imperfection, but there are certain transgressions or certain consequences of transgressions that can degrade man absolutely. These are *original sins* of the second order, but which evoke the first for us, however imperfectly. From this origin come savages, about whom so many extravagant things have been said, and who served as the eternal text for J.-J. Rousseau, one of the most dangerous sophists of our century, and yet the one who was the most deprived of true knowledge, wisdom, and especially of profundity, with only an apparent depth that was all a matter of words. He constantly mistook the savage for the primitive man, although the savage is and can only be the descendant of a man detached from the great tree of civilization by some transgression, but of a genre that can no longer be repeated, so far as we can judge, for I doubt new savages will be formed.

As a consequence of the same error, the languages of these savages have been taken for primitive languages, whereas they are and could only be the debris of ancient languages, *ruined*, if I may put it that way, and degraded, like the men who speak them. In effect, every individual or national degradation is immediately heralded by a rigorously proportional degradation in language. How could man lose an idea or merely the correctness of an

Extracts from *Second Dialogue*

idea without losing the word or the accuracy of the word that expresses it? And how, on the contrary, could he extend or sharpen his thinking without this advance being displayed immediately in his language?

So there is an *original illness* just as there is an original sin; which is to say that in virtue of this primitive degradation, we are all subject to all sorts of physical sufferings in *general*; just as in virtue of this degradation we are all subject to all sorts of vices in *general*. This original illness has no other name. It is only the capacity to suffer all kinds of illnesses, just as original sin (abstraction made of imputation) is only the capacity to commit all kinds of crimes, which completes the comparison.

But there are, moreover, original illnesses of the second order, just as there are *original* transgressions of the second order. Which is to say that certain transgressions committed by certain men can degrade them anew *more or less*, and thus be perpetuated more or less like illnesses in the vices of their descendants. It may be that these great transgressions are no longer possible, but it is nonetheless true that the general principle subsists, and that the Christian religion showed itself in possession of great secrets when it turned its whole attention and all the force of its legislative and teaching power to the legitimate reproduction of men to prevent every deadly transmission from fathers to children. If I did not distinguish the illnesses that we owe immediately to personal crimes from those that we owe to the sins of our fathers, the fault is slight, since as I told you a little while ago, they are all in truth punishments for crime. This heredity shocks human reason at first, but until we can talk of the matter at greater length, let us content ourselves with the general rule that I pointed out at the beginning: *all beings that reproduce will only produce what resembles themselves.*

Here, Senator, I invoke your *intellectual conscience*. If a man indulges in such crimes or such a series of crimes that they were capable of altering the moral principle within him, you understand that this degradation is transmissible, just as you understand the transmission of scrofulous or syphilitic vice. For the rest, I have no need of these hereditary evils. Look at all that I have said on this subject as a conversational parenthesis; all the rest remains unshakeable. In summing up all the considerations that I have put before you, there remains, I hope, no doubt *that the innocent man, when he suffers, suffers only in his quality as a man; and that the immense majority of evils fall on crime.* This is all I need for the moment. Now . . .

The Chevalier

For me at least, it would be quite useless for you to go any further; for since you spoke of savages I have not been listening to you. In speaking about this kind of men, you mentioned, in passing, something that has kept me completely occupied. Are you really able to prove to me that the languages of savages are the *remnants* and not the *rudiments* of languages?

Extracts from *Second Dialogue*

The Count

If I wanted to undertake this proof seriously, Chevalier, I would first have to prove to you that it would be up to you to prove the contrary; but I fear that this would involve me in a dissertation that would be much too long. If, however, the importance of the subject appears to you to merit my exposing my *faith* to you, I will do this willingly and without details for your future reflections. Here is what I believe on the principal points of which a simple consequence has caught your attention.

The essence of all intelligence is to know and to love. The limits of its knowledge are those of its nature. The immortal being learns nothing; he knows by nature all he must know. On the other hand, no intelligent being can love evil naturally or in virtue of its essence; for that God would have to have created it evil, which is impossible. If therefore man is subject to ignorance or evil, this can only be in virtue of an accidental degradation, which can only be the consequence of a crime. This need, this hunger for knowledge, which agitates man, is only the natural tendency of his being, which carries him towards his original state and alerts him to what he is. He *gravitates*, if I may so express myself, towards the regions of light. No beaver, no swallow, no bee wants to know more than its predecessors. All these beings are happy in the place they occupy. All are degraded, but are ignorant of it; man alone senses his degradation, and this feeling is at once the proof of his greatness and of his misery, of his sublime prerogatives, and of his incredible degradation. In the state to which he is reduced he has not even the sad happiness of being unaware of himself; he must ceaselessly contemplate himself, and he cannot contemplate himself without blushing; his very greatness humiliates him, since the enlightenment that raises him as high as angels only serves to show him the abominable tendencies within himself degrading him to the level of the brutes. He searches in the depth of his being for some healthy part without being able to find it: evil has soiled everything, *and the whole of man is only a disease.* An inconceivable combination of two different and incompatible powers, a monstrous centaur, he feels that he is the result of some unknown crime, some detestable mixture that has vitiated man even in his deepest essence.

Every intellect is by its very nature the result, single yet in three parts, of a *perception* that apprehends, a *reason* that affirms, and a *will* that acts. The first two powers are only weakened in man, but the third *is broken*, and like Tasso's serpent, *it drags itself behind itself*, completely ashamed of its painful impotence. It is in the third power that man senses himself fatally wounded. He does not know what he wants; he wants what he does not want; he does not want what he wants; he *would want to want*. He sees in himself something that is not himself and that is stronger than himself. The wise man resists and cries out: *Who will deliver me?* The fool obeys, and calls his cowardice *happiness*; but he cannot get rid of this other incorruptible will in his nature, although it has lost its power; and remorse, piercing his heart, never ceases to

Extracts from *Second Dialogue*

cry out to him: *By doing what you do not want, you acknowledge the law.* Who could believe that such a being could have left the hands of the Creator in such a state? This idea is so revolting, that philosophy alone, I mean pagan philosophy, hit on original sin. Did not old Timon of Locris already say, after his master Pythagoras surely, *that our vices come less from ourselves than from our fathers and the elements of which we are made?* Did not Plato even say *that what one must take into account is the generator* rather than the *generated?* And in another place did he not add that *the Lord, God of Gods, seeing that all beings subject to generation have lost* (or had destroyed in them) *the inestimable gift, had decided to subject them to a treatment suited at the same time to punish them and regenerate them.* Cicero did not distance himself from the feeling of these philosophers and of those initiates who had thought *that we are in this world to expiate certain crimes committed in another.* He even cited and adopted part of Aristotle's comparison, in which the contemplation of human nature reminded him of the dreadful punishment of a wretch tied to a cadaver and condemned to rot with it. Elsewhere he said expressly *that nature had treated us like a step-mother rather than as a mother, and that the divine spirit in us is as if stifled by the tendency we have within us for all the vices,* and is it not a singular fact that Ovid spoke of man in precisely the same terms as St Paul? The erotic poet said: *I see what is good, I love it, and evil seduces me*; and the apostle so elegantly translated by Racine said:

> I do not the good that I love,
> And I do the evil that I hate.

Moreover, when the philosophers whom I have just cited assure us that the vices of human nature pertain more *to the fathers than to the children*, clearly they are not speaking of any generation in particular. If the proposition remains vague, it makes no sense, so that the very nature of things relates it to a corruption that is original and in consequence universal. Plato tells us *that in contemplating himself, he does not know if he sees a monster more duplicitous and more evil than Typhon, or rather a moral, gentle, and benevolent being who partakes in the nature of the divinity.* He adds that man, so torn in opposite directions, cannot act well or live happily *without reducing to servitude that power of the soul in which evil resides, and without setting free* that which is the home and *the agent of virtue.* This is precisely the Christian doctrine, and one could not confess more clearly the doctrine of original sin.

What do words matter? Man is evil, horribly evil. Did God create him this way? No, undoubtedly, and Plato himself hastens to reply *that the good being neither wishes nor does evil to anyone*. So we are degraded – but how? This corruption that Plato saw in himself does not appear to have been something particular to his person, and surely he did not believe himself worse than his fellow men. So he was saying essentially what David had said: *My mother conceived me in iniquity*, and if these words had occurred to him he would have adopted them without difficulty. Moreover, since all degradation can only be a punishment, and all punishment presupposes a crime, reason alone finds itself led forcefully to original sin. Since our deadly inclination towards evil is a truth of feeling and experience proclaimed in every century, and since this inclination is always more or less victorious over conscience, and since the laws have never ceased to produce transgressions of all kinds on this earth, man can never recognize and deplore this sad state without confessing at the same time the lamentable dogma that I have been expounding to you, for man cannot be *wicked* without being *evil*, nor evil without being degraded, nor degraded without being punished, nor punished without being guilty.

In short, gentlemen, there is nothing so well attested, nothing so universally believed in one form or other, nothing, finally, so intrinsically plausible as the theory of original sin.

Let me add one more thing. I hope you will have no difficulty in appreciating that an originally degraded intelligence is and remains incapable (barring a substantial regeneration) of that ineffable contemplation that our old teachers very appropriately called the *beatific vision*, since it produces, and even is, eternal happiness, just as you can understand that a material eye that is seriously injured can remain incapable in this state of enduring the light of the sun. Now this incapacity of enjoying the SUN, is, if I am not mistaken, the only consequence of original sin that we should regard as natural and independent of any actual transgression. It seems to me that reason can reach this far, and I believe it has a right to applaud itself for this, without ceasing to be docile.

Such is man studied in himself; let us pass on to his history.

All of humanity is descended from one couple. This

truth, like every other, has been denied. So what are we to make of this?

We know very little about the time before the Flood, and according to some plausible conjectures, it will never be granted us to know more. Only one consideration is of interest to us and we should never lose sight of it: this is that punishments are always proportional to crimes, and crimes are always proportional to the knowledge of the guilty – so that the Flood presupposes unheard of crimes and these crimes assume knowledge infinitely higher than that which we possess today. This is what is certain and what must be more deeply studied. In the righteous family, this knowledge, freed from the evil that rendered it so deadly, survived the destruction of humanity. With respect to the nature and direction of science, we are blinded by a glaring sophism that has fascinated everyone: this sophism lies in judging the age in which men saw effects in causes by that in which they rise painfully from effects to causes, in which they even concern themselves only with effects, in which they say it is useless to concern oneself with causes, and in which they do not even know what a cause is. They never cease to repeat: *Think of the time that it took to know such and such a thing!* What inconceivable blindness! It only took a moment. If man could understand the cause of a single physical phenomenon, he could probably understand all the others. We do not want to see that the most difficult to discover truths are easy to understand. The solution of the problem of the *annulus* once brought a thrill of joy to the best geometer of antiquity, but this solution is found in every elementary mathematics textbook, and does not surpass the intellectual capacity of a fifteen-year old.

Plato, speaking somewhere of what is most important for man to know, suddenly adds with the penetrating simplicity natural to him: *These things are learned easily and perfectly IF SOMEONE TEACHES THEM TO US*. This is exactly the case. It is, moreover, obviously apparent that the first men who repeopled the world after the great catastrophe would have needed extraordinary assistance to succeed against the difficulties of all kinds that faced them. And see, gentlemen, the beautiful character of the truth! Is it a question of proving it? Witnesses come and present themselves from every side; they have never been silent and they have never contradicted themselves, whereas the witnesses of error contradict themselves, even when they are lying. Listen to what wise antiquity has to say about the first men: it will tell you that they were marvellous men, and that beings of a superior order deigned to favour them with the most precious communications. On this point there is no discord: initiates, philosophers, poets, history, fable, Asia and Europe, speak with one voice. Such agreement of reason, revelation, and every human tradition forms a demonstration that cannot be contradicted. So not only did men begin with science, but with a science different from our own, and superior to our own because it had a higher origin, which is what made it more dangerous. And this explains why science was always considered mysterious in principle, and why it was always confined to the temples, where the flame finally burned out when it could serve no purpose but to burn.

Joseph de Maistre

Not counting the first outlines of science, no one knows how far back to date certain great institutions, profound knowledge, and some magnificent monuments to human industry and human power. Near the site of St Peter's in Rome we find the great sewer of the Tarquins and certain Cyclopean constructions. This epoch goes back to the Etruscans, whose arts and sciences are lost in antiquity, whom Hesiod called *great and illustrious* nine centuries before Jesus Christ, who established colonies in Greece and on numerous islands several centuries before the Trojan War. Pythagoras, travelling in Greece six centuries before the Christian era, learned there the cause of all the phenomena of Venus. It is from him, too, that we learn something even more curious, since all antiquity knew *that Mercury, to save a goddess from great embarrassment, played dice with the moon, and won from her the seventy-second part of the day.* I even admit to you that in reading the *Banquet of the Seven Sages* in the *Moralia* of Plutarch, I could not help suspecting that the Egyptians knew the true form of planetary orbits. You can, when you like, give yourself the pleasure of verifying this text. Julian [the Apostate], in one of his tasteless discourses (I don't know which one), calls the sun *the god of the seven rays*. Where did he find this singular epithet? Certainly it could only have come to him from the ancient Asiatic traditions that he would have collected in his theurgic studies; and the sacred books of India give a good commentary on this text, since one reads there that seven virgins assembled to celebrate the coming of *Krishna*, who is the Indian Apollo, the god appearing all at once in the middle of them and proposing to them that they dance; but the virgins excusing themselves for lack of dancers, the god provided for them by dividing himself, so that each girl had her *Krishna*. Add that the true system of the world was perfectly known in the most remote antiquity. Think of the pyramids of Egypt, rigorously oriented, preceding all the known epochs of history; that the arts are brothers that live and shine together; that the nation that was able to create colours capable of resisting the free action of the air for thirty centuries, raised to a height of six hundred feet weights that would defy all our mechanics, sculpted in granite birds whose species the modern traveller can recognize; this nation, I say, was *necessarily* also as eminent in the other arts, and even knew *necessarily* a host of things that we do not know. If I cast my eyes on Asia, I see the walls of Nemrod raised on an earth still wet from the flood, and astronomical observatories as old as the city. So where will we place the so-called times of barbarism and ignorance? Amusing philosophers tell us: *We lack centuries*. They are very much lacking for you, since the epoch of the Flood is there to smother all the romances of the imagination; and the geological observations that demonstrate the fact of the Flood also demonstrate its date with a limited uncertainty in time as insignificant as that which remains with respect to the distance to the moon in space. Even Lucretius could not prevent himself from rendering a striking testimony to the newness of the human family. And physics, which can pass for history in this case, draws from this a new support, since we see that historical certitude ends for all nations at the same time, this is to say towards the eighth century before our era. Let those people who believe everything except the Bible cite for us Chinese observations made four or five thousand years ago, on an earth that did not yet exist, by a people for whom the Jesuits had to make almanacs at the end of the sixteenth century.

All this merits no more discussion; let them talk. I only want to present you with one observation that perhaps you have not made: this is that the whole system of Indian antiquities has been overthrown from top to bottom by the useful labours of the Calcutta Academy, and the simple inspection of a geographical map demonstrating that China could not have been inhabited before India, the same blow that strikes Indian antiquities has tumbled those of China, on which Voltaire especially never ceased to bore us.

For the rest, since Asia has been the theatre of the greatest marvels, it is not surprising that its peoples have kept a liking for the marvellous that is stronger than that which is natural for men in general, and which each can recognize in himself. It is because of this that they have always shown so little taste and talent for the *conclusions* of our sciences. One could say that they still recall that primitive science was an era of *intuitions*. Does a bound eagle ask for a *mongolfière* [hot air balloon] to ascend into the sky. No, it only asks that its bonds be loosened. And who knows if these people are not yet destined to contemplate spectacles that are refused to the quibbling genius of Europe?

Whatever happens, notice, I beg you, that it is impossible to think of modern science without seeing it constantly surrounded by all the machines of the mind and all the methods of its art. Under skimpy northern dress, his head lost in the curls of deceptive locks, his arms loaded with books and instruments of all kinds, pale from long nights and work, the modern scientist drags himself along the road to truth, soiled with ink and panting, always bending his algebra-furrowed brow towards the earth. There was nothing like this in high antiquity. In so far as it is possible to perceive the science of early times at such a distance, one always sees it free and isolated, soaring rather than walking, and presenting in its whole being something airy and supernatural. Exposing to the winds the hair that escapes from an oriental *mitre*, an *ephod* covering a breast uplifted with inspiration, it looked only to the heavens, and its disdainful foot seemed to touch the earth only to leave it. However, although it demanded nothing of anyone and seemed to know no human support, it is no less proven that it possessed the rarest knowledge. This is the great proof, if you really think about it, that antique science was dispensed from the labour imposed on ours, and that nothing could be more mistaken than all the calculations on which we base our modern experiments.

The Chevalier

You have just proved to us, good friend, that one speaks willingly of what one loves. You promised me a dry symbol, but your profession of faith has become a kind of dissertation. What is good in it, is that you have not said a word about those savages who started us off.

The Count

I confess to you that on this point I am like Job, *full of speeches*. I willingly pour them out before you; but I cannot, though it cost me my life, be understood by all men or make them believe me. In any case, I don't know why you bring me back to savages. Really, it seems to me that I have never stopped speaking to you of them, even for a moment. If all humanity is descended from the three couples who repopulated the world, and if humanity began with science, the savage can only be, as I have told you, a detached branch of the social tree. Although it is incontestable, I could even abandon the argument from science, and restrict myself to religion, which alone suffices, though only very imperfectly, to exclude the state of savagery. Wherever you find an altar, there civilization is to be found. *The poor man in his cabin, covered with straw* is undoubtedly less learned than we are, but more truly social if he learns his catechism and profits from it. The most shameful errors and the most detestable cruelties soil the annals of Memphis, Athens, and Rome, but all the virtues together honour the cabins of Paraguay [the Jesuit missions]. Moreover, if the religion of Noah's family must necessarily have been the most enlightened and the most vital that it is possible to imagine, and if it is in this very reality that the causes of its corruption must be sought, this second

Extracts from *Second Dialogue*

demonstration added to the first surpasses it. Thus we must recognize that the state of civilization and knowledge is in a certain sense the natural and primitive state of man. As well, all oriental traditions begin with a state of perfection and enlightenment, what I again call *supernatural enlightenment*; and even Greece, deceitful Greece, *which dared everything in history*, rendered homage to this truth by placing its age of gold at the beginnings of things. It is no less remarkable that it did not attribute the savage state to the following ages, even to the age of iron. So that all that they have told us about the first men living in the woods, feeding themselves on acorns, and passing finally to the social state, puts them in contradiction with themselves, and can only be supported with respect to particular cases, this is to say some tribes that have been degraded and then painfully returned to *the state of nature*, that is to say, to civilization. Did not Voltaire, and that says everything, admit that the motto of every nation has always been: THE AGE OF GOLD WAS THE FIRST TO BE SEEN ON THE EARTH. So then, all nations have protested in concert against the hypothesis of an original state of barbarism, and surely this protest counts for something.

Now what does it matter to me to date the point at which such and such a branch was separated from the tree? That it did suffices for me. There is no doubt about the degradation, and I dare to say as well, no doubt about the cause of the degradation, which can only have been a crime. Some leader having altered a people's moral principle by some of those transgressions, which following appearances are no longer possible in the present state of things because happily we no longer know enough to become so guilty, this leader, I say, transmitted the anathema to his posterity; and since every constant force accelerates by its very nature since it is always acting on itself, this degradation bearing on his descendants without interruption has finally made them into what we call savages. It is this final degree of brutalization that Rousseau and his like call *the state of nature*.

Two extremely different causes have thrown a deceptive cloud around the frightful state of the savages; the one is ancient, the other belongs to our own century. In the first place, the immense charity of the Catholic priesthood in speaking to us of these men has often placed its desires in place of reality. There was only too much truth in the first reaction of Europeans, in the time of Columbus, to refuse to recognize as equals the degraded men who peopled the new world. The priests used all their influence to contradict this opinion, which was too favourable to the barbarous despotism of the new masters. They cried out to the Spaniards: 'No violence, the Gospel forbids it; if you do not know how to overthrow the idols in the hearts of these unfortunate beings, what good is it to overthrow their miserable altars? To make them know and love God requires other tactics and other weapons.' From deserts watered with their own sweat and blood, they made their way to Madrid and Rome to ask for edicts and bulls against the pitiless greed that wanted to enslave the Indians. The merciful priest exalted them to make them precious; he played down the evil, he exaggerated the good, he promised what he hoped would be. Finally Robertson, who is not suspect, warns us, in his history of America, *that on this subject it is necessary to distrust all those writers belonging to the clergy, since, in general, they are too favourable to the natives.*

Another source of false judgements with respect to the Indians can be found in contemporary philosophy, which has used these savages to prop up its vain and culpable declamations against the social order. But the slightest attention is sufficient to keep us on guard against the errors of both charity and bad faith. One cannot glance at the savage without reading the curse that is written not only on his soul but even on the exterior form of his body. This is a deformed child, robust and ferocious, on whom the light of intelligence casts no more than a pale and flickering beam. A formidable hand weighing on these benighted races effaces in them the two distinctive characters of our greatness, foresight and perfectibility. The savage cuts down the tree to gather its fruit, he unharnesses the ox that missionaries have just given him, and cooks it with the wood of the plough. He has known us for three centuries without having wanted anything from us, except gunpowder to kill his fellows and brandy to kill himself. Yet he has never learned to make these things; he relies on our greed, which will never fail him.

Just as the most abject and revolting substances are nevertheless still capable of a certain degradation, so are the natural vices of humanity even more vicious in the savage. He is a thief, he is cruel, he is dissolute; but he is these things in a different way than we are. To become criminals we must overcome our nature; the savage follows his. He has an appetite for crime, and no remorse at all. While the son kills his father to spare him the inconvenience of old age, his woman destroys in her womb the fruit of their brutal lust to escape the fatigue of nursing it. He rips off the bleeding scalp of his living enemy; he tears him to pieces, roasts him, and devours him while singing. If he comes upon strong liquor, he drinks to intoxication, to fever, to death, deprived equally of the reason that would command a man to fear it and of the instinct that warns the animal by distaste. He is visibly perverted; he has been stricken in the deepest layers of his moral being. He makes the observer who knows how to see tremble. But do we want to tremble for ourselves and in a very salutary way? Let us reflect that with our intelligence, our morals, our sciences, and our arts, we are to the primitive man precisely what the savage is to us.

[. . .]

Seventh Dialogue

The Chevalier

This time, Senator, I hope you will keep your promise, and tell us something about war.

The Senator

I am quite ready to do so, for this is a subject on which I have meditated a great deal. I have been thinking about war ever since I began to think; this terrible subject has seized my full attention, and yet I have never gone into it deeply enough.

The first thing I am going to tell you will undoubtedly astonish you, but for me it is an incontestable truth: *'Given man with his reason, his feelings, and his affections, there is no way of explaining how war is humanly possible.'* This is my well considered opinion. Somewhere La Bruyère describes this great human absurdity with all his characteristic energy. It was many years ago when I read this piece, but I still recall it perfectly. He insists strongly on the folly of war; yet, the more foolish it is, the less explicable.

Joseph de Maistre

The Chevalier

However it seems to me that one can say quite briefly: *kings order you, and you must march.*

The Senator

Oh! Not at all, my dear Chevalier, I assure you that this is not the case. Every time that a man who is not an absolute fool presents you with a question he considers very problematic after giving it careful thought, distrust those quick answers that come to the mind of someone who has considered it only briefly or not at all. These answers are usually simplistic views lacking in consistency, which explain nothing, or which do not bear examination. Sovereigns command effectively and in a lasting way only within the circle of things acknowledged by opinion, and they are not the ones who trace the circle of opinion. In every country there are much less shocking things than war that a sovereign would never venture to command. Remember the joke that you told me one day about a nation *that has an academy of sciences, an astronomical observatory, and a faulty calendar*. More seriously, you also told me that you heard one of this nation's statesmen say *that he would not be at all sure about innovating on this last issue; and that under the last government, so distinguished by liberal ideas* (as they say today), *they never dared undertake this change*. You even asked me what I thought about it. Be that as it may, you

Seventh Dialogue

see that there are subjects much less essential than war on which the authorities sense that they must not commit themselves; and note carefully, I beg you, that is not a question of explaining the *possibility* of war, but its *facility*.

To cut beards off and to shorten robes, Peter the Great needed all the strength of his invincible personality; but to lead innumerable legions onto the field of battle, even at a time *when he was being defeated to learn how to defeat*, he, like any other ruler, only needed to say the word. Yet there is in man, despite his immense degradation, an element of love drawing him towards his fellow men; compassion is as natural to him as breathing. By what inconceivable magic is he always ready, at the first beat of the drum, to cast off this sacred character and to be off without resistance, often even with a certain elation (which also has its own peculiar character), to blow to pieces on the battlefield a brother who has never offended him, and who on his side advances to do the same thing to him if he can? I could conceive of a national war, but how many such wars have there been? One in a thousand years, perhaps; for the rest, among civilized nations especially, who reflect on it and know what they are doing, I confess I don't understand it at all. It could be said that *glory explains everything*; but, in the first place, glory only goes to the leaders; in the second place, this only evades the difficulty, for then I must ask precisely why this extraordinary glory is attached to war.

I have often had a vision that I would like to share with you. I imagine that a stranger to our planet comes here for some *sufficient* reason, and talks to one of us about the order that reigns in this world. Among the

Joseph de Maistre

curious things that are recounted to him, he is told that corruption and vices, about which he has been fully informed, in certain circumstances require men to die by the hand of men, and that we restrict this right to kill legally to the executioner and to the soldier. He will also be told: 'The first brings death to convicted and condemned criminals, and these executions are so rare fortunately, that one of these ministers of death suffices for each province. As for soldiers, there are never enough of them for they kill without restraint, and they always kill honest men. Of these two professional *killers*, the soldier and the executioner, the one is greatly honoured, and has always been so honoured among the peoples that up to the present have inhabited this planet to which you have come. The other, on the contrary, has just as generally been declared infamous. Can you guess on which one the condemnation falls?'

Surely this travelling spirit would not hesitate for a moment; he would accord the executioner all the praise that you could not refuse him the other day, Count, despite all our prejudices, when you spoke to us of this *gentleman*, as Voltaire would have said. 'This sublime being,' he would have told us, 'is the cornerstone of society; since crime has become habitual on your earth, and since it can only be arrested by punishment, if you deprive the world of the executioner all order will disappear with him. Moreover, what greatness of soul, what noble disinterestedness must necessarily be assumed to exist in a man who devotes himself to functions that are undoubtedly worthy of respect, but which are so trying and contrary to your nature! For, since I

Seventh Dialogue

have been among you, I have noticed that it distresses you to kill a chicken in cold blood. I am therefore persuaded that opinion surrounds him with all the honour that he needs and that is justly due him. As for the soldier, he is, all things considered, an agent of cruelty and injustice. How many obviously just wars have there been? How many obviously unjust! How many individual injustices, horrors, and useless atrocities! So I imagine that opinion among you has very justly poured as much shame on the head of the soldier as it has poured glory on that of the impartial executor of the judgement of sovereign justice.'

You know what the situation really is, gentlemen, and how mistaken the spirit would be! In fact, the serviceman and the executioner occupy the two extremities of the social scale, but at quite the opposite ends from this fine theory. There is nothing so noble as the first, nothing so abject as the second; I would not be indulging in a play on words by saying that their functions only approach each other in diverging; they touch each other in the same way that in a circle 1° touches 360°, precisely because they cannot be farther apart. The soldier is so noble that he even ennobles what public opinion regards as the most ignoble, since he can exercise the functions of an executioner without debasing himself, provided however that he only executes his fellow soldiers and that he uses only his weapons for this purpose.

Joseph de Maistre

The Chevalier

Ah, what you have said is important, my dear friend! In any country where, for any reason whatsoever, a soldier is ordered to execute criminals who are not soldiers, in a twinkling of an eye, and without apparent reason, all the glory that surrounds the serviceman will disappear. He will still be feared, no doubt, for any man who is always armed with a good rifle merits great respect; but the indefinable aura of honour will be irretrievably lost. The officer will no longer be anything as an officer; if he is a man of birth and merit, he can still be well thought of, *despite* his rank rather than *because* of it. He would ennoble it instead of being ennobled by it; and if his rank provides a large salary, he would enjoy the consideration of wealth, but never that of nobility. As you have said, Senator, '*provided however that he only executes his fellow soldiers and that he uses only his weapons for this purpose.*' Moreover we must add: *provided that it is a question of a military crime*; once it is a question of a *common* crime, it is a matter for the executioner.

The Count

In fact, this is the custom. Ordinary courts having jurisdiction over civil crimes, soldiers guilty of such crimes are sent before them. However, if it pleased the sovereign to order otherwise, I am far from thinking it certain that the character of the soldier would suffer by it.

Seventh Dialogue

Nevertheless we are all three agreed on the other two conditions, and we do not doubt that his character would be irreversibly tarnished if he were ordered to shoot a simple civilian or to put his comrade to death by burning or hanging. For maintenance of the honour and discipline of any group or association, privileged rewards have less effect than privileged punishments. The Romans, who were at once the most sensitive and the most warlike people in antiquity, came up with a singular idea with respect to simple correction in military discipline. Believing that there could be no discipline without a stick, and nevertheless not wanting to debase either the one who strikes or the one who is struck, they thought of consecrating military beatings in a certain way. For this purpose they chose the wood that was the most useless for anything else, the vine branch, and designated it uniquely for the punishment of soldiers. The vine branch in the hand of the centurion was the sign of his authority and the instrument of non-capital corporal punishment. In general, among the Romans the military beating was a penalty acknowledged by the law. However, no non-military person could be struck with a vine branch, and no other wood other than that of the vine could be used to strike a soldier. I don't know why some similar idea has never occurred to a modern sovereign. If I were consulted on this matter, my thought would not go back to the vine, since servile imitations are worthless; I would propose the laurel.

Joseph de Maistre

The Chevalier

Your idea enchants me, the more so in that I think it quite capable of being put into execution. I assure you that I would very willingly present to His Imperial Majesty a plan for a large greenhouse, which would be established in the capital, and devoted exclusively to growing the laurel required to furnish sticks for all the junior officers in the Russian army. This greenhouse would be under the supervision of an officer in charge, a Chevalier of St George of at least second class, who would carry the title of *high inspector of the laurel greenhouse*; the plants would be cared for, worked, and cut by old veterans of unblemished reputations. The model stick, of which all others would have to be rigorous copies, would be kept in the war office in a silver-gilt case; each stick would be suspended from the junior officer's buttonhole by a ribbon of St George. And over the door of the greenhouse one would read: *This is my wood, which produces my foliage*. In truth, this nonsense would not be the least stupid. The only thing that embarrasses me a bit is that the corporals . . .

The Senator

My dear young friend, any genius whatsoever, in any country there might be, would find it impossible, without stopping for breath, to produce a *Code* without a single fault, even if it were only a question of a *stick code*. So, while you allow your idea to ripen a bit, permit me to continue.

Although the military is in itself dangerous to the well being and liberty of every nation, because the motto of this profession will always be, more or less, that of Achilles, *Jura nego mihi nata* [I claim that for me no laws exist], nevertheless the nations most jealous of their liberties have never thought differently than the rest of mankind about the pre-eminence of the military profession. Antiquity thought no differently than we do on this point; it is one of those on which men have always agreed and always will. So this is the problem I want to pose for you: *Explain why the most honourable thing in the world, according to the judgement of all of humanity, without exception, has always been the right to shed innocent blood innocently?* If you look at the matter closely, you will see that there is something mysterious and inexplicable in the extraordinary value that men have always attached to military glory, the more so in that, if we took into account only theory and human reasoning, we would be led to directly opposite ideas. So it is not a question of explaining the possibility of war by the glory that surrounds it, but of explaining this glory itself, which is not easy.

I would also like to share you with another idea on the same subject. We have been told a thousand and one times that, since nations are in a state of nature with respect to one another, they can only settle their differences by war. Since I am in a questioning mood, I will also ask: *why has every nation remained in a state of nature with respect to every other without ever making a single try, a single attempt, to break out of it?* According to the foolish doctrines in which we were nurtured, there was a time when men did not live in society; this imaginary state was ridiculously called the *state of nature*. They add that men, having wisely weighed the advantages of the two states, chose the one that we see . . .

The Count

Allow me to interrupt you for a moment to share with you an argument that comes to my mind against this doctrine, which you have so rightly called *foolish*. The savage holds so strongly to his most brutal habits that nothing can break him of them. You have undoubtedly seen, at the head of the *Discourse on the Inequality of Conditions*, the engraving based on the true or false anecdote of the Hottentot who returns to his fellows. Rousseau little suspected that this frontispiece was a powerful argument against his book. The savage sees our arts, laws, sciences, luxuries, pleasures of every kind, and especially our superiority, from which he cannot hide and yet which would excite some desires in hearts that were capable of it; but all this does not even tempt him, and continually *he returns to his fellows*. If the savage of our own time, knowledgeable about both states and being able to compare them daily in certain countries, remains resolutely in his own, how can it be imagined that the primitive savage emerged from his by means of deliberation to pass into another state of which he had no knowledge? Therefore society is as old as man; therefore the savage is and can only be a degraded and punished man. In truth, I see nothing as clear for unadulterated good sense.

The Senator

You are preaching to the converted, as the saying goes, but I thank you for your argument; one never has too many weapons against error. But to return to what I was just saying, if man passed from *the state of nature*, in the common usage of the term, to the state of civilization, either by deliberation or *by accident* (I am still speaking the language of the foolish), why have nations not had as much wit or luck as individuals, and how is it that they have never agreed to establish a general society to bring an end to national quarrels in the same way that men have agreed to establish a national sovereign in order to bring an end to the quarrels of individuals? It is easy to ridicule *the impracticable peace of the Abbé Saint-Pierre* (and I agree that it was impracticable), but I ask why this is so, why nations have been unable to raise themselves to the social state like individuals, and how it is that reasoning Europe, above all, has never attempted anything of this kind?

In particular, I would address this same question to believers with still more confidence. How is it that God, who is the author of the society of individuals, has never permitted man, his cherished creature who has received the divine attribute of perfectibility, even to attempt to elevate himself to a society of nations? Every possible argument for showing that such a society is impossible militates in the same way against a society of individuals. The argument drawn principally from the impracticable universality that would have to be given to the great sovereign holds no force, since it is false that it would have to include the whole world. Nations are sufficiently distinguished and divided by rivers, seas, mountains, and religions, and especially by languages that have a greater or lesser affinity. If even a certain number of nations agreed together to enter *the state of civilization*, this would already be a great step in favour of humanity. Other nations, you might say, would attack them. Well, so what? They would always be more peaceful among themselves and stronger than the others, which would be sufficient. Perfection is not at all necessary on this point; it would already be a great deal even to approach it. I cannot persuade myself that nothing of this sort had ever been attempted, if it were not for an occult and terrible law demanding human blood.

The Count

You took it as an undeniable fact that this *civilization of nations* has never been attempted, yet in truth it has often been tried and even stubbornly – true without it being known that this is what was being attempted, which was a circumstance very favourable for its success – and it has even been close to succeeding, at least in so far as the imperfection of our nature allows. However, men made mistakes: they took one thing for another,

Seventh Dialogue

and everything failed, from all appearances, because of this occult and terrible law of which you spoke.

The Senator

I would ask you several questions if I were not afraid of losing the thread of my ideas. So please observe, I beg you, a phenomenon well worth your attention, which is that the profession of arms, as we might think or fear if we were not instructed by experience, does not in the least tend to degrade, brutalize, or harden those who follow it – on the contrary, it tends to improve them. The most honest man is usually the honest soldier, and for my part I have always been partial, as I told you before, to military good sense, which I very much prefer to the long-windedness of businessmen. In the ordinary commerce of life, military men are more likeable, easier to get along with, and often, it appears to me, more obliging than other men. In the midst of political conflicts they are generally intrepid defenders of the old maxims, and the most dazzling sophistries are usually defeated by their uprightness. They willingly occupy themselves with useful things and useful knowledge, such as political economy, for example. Perhaps the only work antiquity has left us on this topic was by a soldier, Xenophon, and the first work of this kind that was produced in France was by another soldier, Marshal Vauban. Among soldiers, religion is allied to honour in a remarkable way, and even when religion reproaches them gravely for their conduct, they do not refuse it the aid of their swords, if it needs them. Much is said about the *licence of camps*. No doubt it is great, but usually soldiers do not find vices in the camps; they carry them there. A moral and austere people always furnishes excellent soldiers, terrible only on the battlefield. Virtues, even piety, combine very well with military courage; far from enfeebling the warrior, these virtues exalt him. St Louis was not inconvenienced by the hairshirt beneath his armour. Even Voltaire agreed in good faith that *an army ready to die in obedience to God would be invincible*. You have no doubt learned from Racine's letters that when he was with Louis XIV's army in 1692, he never attended Mass in the camp without seeing some musketeer communicating with the greatest edification.

Look up in Fénelon's *Oeuvres spirituelles* the letter he wrote to an officer among his friends. Heartbroken at not being employed in the army, as he had flattered himself he should, this man had been led, probably by Fénelon, into the ways of the highest perfection: he had achieved *pure love* and *the death* [of self] *of the Mystics*. Now perhaps you would think that the tender and loving soul of the *swan of Cambrai* would find compensations for his friend in the scenes of carnage in which he no longer had to take part; that he would say: *After all, you are lucky, you are no longer seeing the horrors of war and the frightful spectacle of all the crimes that it involves*. He carefully avoids such cowardly considerations; on the contrary, he consoles him and grieves with him. He sees in this privation an overwhelming misfortune, a bitter cross, completely suitable for detaching his friend from the world.

Seventh Dialogue

What do we say of this other officer, to whom Madame Guyon wrote that he must not worry if he sometimes had to miss Mass on working days, *especially in the army*? The writers from whom we have these anecdotes, however, lived in a passably warlike century, it seems to me. In short, nothing in this world agrees better than the religious spirit and the military spirit.

The Chevalier

I am very far from contradicting this truth. However, it must be admitted that if virtue does not harm military courage, it can at least be bypassed by the latter, since we have seen, in certain periods, legions of atheists obtain prodigious successes.

The Senator

Why not, I ask you, if these atheists are fighting other atheists? However, allow me to continue. Not only does the military profession ally itself very well with morality in general, but what is quite extraordinary is that it does not in the least weaken those gentle virtues that seem to be most opposed to the profession of arms. The gentlest characters love war, desire war, and go to war with passion. At the first call, this likeable young man, brought up with a horror of violence and blood, rushes from his father's house, his weapons at hand, and seeks on the battlefield what he calls *the enemy*, without yet knowing what *an enemy* is. Yesterday he would have been ill if he had accidentally killed his sister's canary; tomorrow you will see him climbing a pile of cadavers *to see farther*, as Charron said. The blood flowing on all sides only inspires him to shed his own and that of others; he inflames himself by degrees until he reaches *an enthusiasm for carnage*.

The Chevalier

You have not exaggerated. Before my twenty-fourth birthday I had seen *the enthusiasm of carnage* three times; I have experienced it myself, and I especially recall a terrible moment when I would have put an entire army to the sword if I had been able.

The Senator

But if, while we are speaking here, someone asked you to grab a white dove with the cold-bloodedness of a cook, then . . .

The Chevalier

What! You make me sick at heart!

Seventh Dialogue

The Senator

This is precisely the phenomenon that I was just telling you about. The terrifying spectacle of carnage does not harden the true warrior. Amid the blood he sheds, he is humane, just as the wife is chaste in the transports of love. Once he has put his sword back in its scabbard, sacred humanity recovers its rights, and perhaps the most exalted and most generous feelings are to be found among soldiers. Remember, Chevalier, France's great century. It was a time when religion, valour, and science had been put in equilibrium, so to speak, and when the result was the beautiful character that everyone unanimously hailed as the model of European character. If the first element is taken away, the ensemble, that is to say all its beauty, disappears. What has not been noticed enough, is how necessary religion is for the whole, and the role that it plays even where frivolous observers might have thought it foreign. The divine spirit, which has particularly blessed Europe, has even mitigated the scourge of eternal justice, and *European war* will always have a special place in annals of the world. Undoubtedly Europeans killed, burned, ravaged, and even, if you wish, committed thousands of useless crimes; but nevertheless they began war in the month of May and ended it in the month of December; they slept under canvas; soldiers fought only soldiers. Whole nations were never at war, and all that was weak was sacred amidst the dreary scenes of this devastating plague.

Joseph de Maistre

It was a magnificent spectacle though to see all the sovereigns of Europe, restrained by I don't know what imperious moderation, never asking of their peoples, even in the moment of greatest peril, all that it would have been possible to obtain from them. They used men gently, and all of them, led by an invisible force, avoided striking killing blows against the sovereignty of the enemy: glory, honour, and eternal praise to the law of love proclaimed unceasingly at the centre of Europe. No nation triumphed over the other; antique war no longer existed except in books or among peoples *seated in the shadow of death*. Fierce wars were ended by a province, a city, often even a few villages, changing masters. Airborne shells avoided royal palaces; more than once dances and spectacles served as interludes for the combatants. The invited enemy officers came to feasts to speak laughingly of the battle that must take place the next day, and even in the horrors of the most bloody clashes, the accents of pity and the formulas of civility greeted the ears of the dying. At the first sign of action, vast hospitals came into being everywhere; medicine, surgery, and pharmacy sent their numerous experts. In the middle of them arose the genius of *St John of God*, of *St Vincent de Paul*, greater, stronger, more than human, constant as faith, active like hope, able as love. All the living victims were collected, treated, and consoled, every wound cared for by the hand of science and charity! . . . A little while ago, Chevalier, you spoke of legions of *atheists* who achieved prodigious successes; I believe that if one could regiment tigers you would see even greater marvels. If you look closely at war, never will Christianity

Seventh Dialogue

appear more sublime, more worthy of divinity, and better suited for men. Moreover, when you said *legions of atheists*, you did not mean it literally; nevertheless suppose these legions to be as bad as they could be, do you know how they could be defeated most easily? It would be by opposing to them the principle diametrically opposed to that by which they are constituted. You can be sure that *legions of atheists* could not stand against *burning legions*.

In short, gentlemen, the functions of the soldier are terrible, but of necessity they belong to a great law of the spiritual world, and we must not be astonished that all the nations of the world have agreed in seeing in this scourge something more particularly divine than others. You may believe that it is not without a great and profound reason that the title GOD OF HOSTS shines forth from all the pages of Holy Scripture. Guilty mortals, and unhappy because we are guilty, we ourselves make necessary all physical evils, but especially war. Men usually lay the blame on rulers, and nothing is more natural: Horace said playfully in this regard:

> By the madness of kings peoples are punished.

J.-B. Rousseau said more seriously and more philosophically:

> It is the wrath of kings that arms the earth,
> It is the wrath of heaven that arms kings.

Notice, moreover, that this law of war, already so terrible, is nevertheless only a chapter in the general law that hangs over the world.

In the vast domain of living things, there reigns an obvious violence, a kind of prescribed rage that arms all creatures to their common doom. As soon as you leave the inanimate kingdom, you find the decree of violent death written on the very frontiers of life. You feel it already in the vegetable kingdom: from the immense catalpa to the humblest herb, how many plants *die*, and how many are *killed*! As soon as you enter the animal kingdom, the law suddenly becomes frighteningly obvious. A power at once hidden and palpable shows itself continually occupied in demonstrating the principle of life by violent means. In each great division of the animal kingdom, it has chosen a certain number of animals charged with devouring the others; thus, there are insects of prey, birds of prey, fish of prey, and quadrupeds of prey. There is no instant of time when some living thing is not being devoured by another.

Above all these numerous animal species is placed man, whose destructive hand spares nothing that lives. He kills to nourish himself, he kills to clothe himself, he kills to adorn himself, he kills to attack, he kills to defend himself, he kills to instruct himself, he kills to amuse himself, he kills to kill: a superb and terrible king, he needs everything and nothing resists him. He knows how many barrels of oil he can get for himself from the head of a shark or a whale; with his sharp pins he mounts for museum display the elegant butterfly he caught in flight on the summit of Mount Blanc or

Seventh Dialogue

Chimborazo; he stuffs the crocodile and embalms the hummingbird; at his command, the rattlesnake dies in preserving fluids to show itself intact to a long line of observers. The horse carrying its master to the tiger hunt struts under the skin of this same animal. Man demands everything at the same time; he takes from the lamb its entrails to make his harp resound, from the whale its bones to stiffen the corset of the young girl, from the wolf its most murderous tooth to polish his pretty works of art, from the elephant its tusks to make a child's toy; his tables are covered with corpses. The philosopher can even discover how this permanent carnage is provided for and ordained in the great scheme of things. But will this law stop at man? Undoubtedly not. Yet who will exterminate him who exterminates everything else? Man! It is man himself who is charged with slaughtering man.

But how can he accomplish this law, he who is a moral and merciful being, who is born to love, who weeps for others as for himself, who finds pleasure in weeping and who even invents fictions to make himself weep, and finally, to whom it has been said that *whoever sheds blood unjustly, by man shall his blood be shed*. It is war that accomplishes the *decree*. Do you not hear the *earth* itself crying out and demanding blood? The blood of animals does not satisfy it, nor even that of criminals spilled by the sword of the law. If human justice struck down all criminals, there would be no war, but it can catch only a few of them, and often it even spares them, without suspecting that this cruel humanity contributes to the necessity of war, especially if at the same time, another blindness no less stupid and no less blind works to extinguish atonement in the world. The *earth* did not cry out in vain; war breaks out. Man, suddenly seized by a *divine* fury foreign to both hatred and anger, goes to the battlefield without knowing what he intends nor even what he is doing. How can this horrible enigma be explained? Nothing is more contrary to man's nature, yet nothing is less repugnant to him; he does with enthusiasm what he holds in horror. Have you never noticed that men never disobey on the field of death. They might well massacre a Nerva or a Henry IV, but what the most abominable tyrant, the most insolent butcher of human flesh, will never hear is: *We no longer want to serve you.* A revolt on the battlefield, an agreement to unite to repudiate a tyrant, is an unheard-of phenomenon. Nothing can resist the force that drags men into combat; an innocent murderer, a passive instrument in a formidable hand: *he plunges head first into the abyss he has dug for himself; he bestows and receives death without suspecting that he himself prepared it.*

Thus, from the maggot up to man, the universal law of the violent destruction of living things is unceasingly fulfilled. The entire earth, perpetually steeped in blood, is nothing but an immense altar on which every living thing must be immolated without end, without restraint, without respite, until the consummation of the world, until the extinction of evil, until the death of death.

But the anathema must strike down man most directly and most visibly: the exterminating angel circles this unhappy globe like the sun, and allows one nation a respite only to strike down others. When crimes, and

Seventh Dialogue

especially crimes of a certain kind, accumulate to a designated point, the angel relentlessly quickens its tireless flight. Like a rapidly turning burning torch, the immense speed of his movement allows him to be simultaneously present everywhere in his formidable orbit. He strikes all the peoples of the earth at the same time. At other times, a minister of a precise and infallible vengeance, he pursues particular nations and bathes them in blood. Do not expect them to make any effort to escape or alleviate their sentence. It is as if we saw these great criminals, enlightened by their consciences, requesting the punishment and accepting it for the sake of their atonement. So long as they have any blood left they will come to offer it, and soon a *sparse youth* will get used to telling of these devastating wars caused by the crimes of their fathers.

War is therefore divine in itself, since it is a law of the world.

War is divine through its consequences of a supernatural nature, which are as much general as particular, consequences little known because little studied, but which are nevertheless incontestable. Who could doubt the great privileges to be found in death in battle? Who could believe that the victims of this dreadful sentence have shed their blood in vain? However, this is not the time to insist on matters of this kind; our century is not yet mature enough to occupy itself with these matters. Let it keep to its physics, but we must nevertheless keep our eyes fixed on the invisible world that will explain everything.

War is divine in the mysterious glory that surrounds

it, and in the no less inexplicable attraction that draws us to it.

War is divine in the protection granted to its great leaders, even the most venturesome, who are rarely struck down in battle, and then only when their reputation can no longer be increased and when their mission has been fulfilled.

War is divine by the way in which it breaks out. I do not want to excuse anyone too easily, but how many of those regarded as the immediate authors of war are themselves carried along by circumstances! At the precise moment caused by men and prescribed by justice, God himself comes forward to avenge the iniquity committed against him by the inhabitants of the world. *The earth, thirsty for blood*, as we heard a few days ago [Second Dialogue], *opens its mouth to receive it and to keep it in its bosom until the time when it must render its account*. So let us applaud as loudly as you wish the worthy poet who cries out:

> To the least interest that would divide
> These blazing sovereigns,
> Bellona [god of war] sustains the reply,
> And saltpetre always announces
> Their willing murderers.

However, these very secondary considerations do not at all prevent us from looking to higher things.

War is divine in its results, which absolutely escape the speculations of human reasons, since they can be totally different for two different nations, even though

Seventh Dialogue

the war appears to have affected them both equally. There are wars that degrade nations, and degrade them for centuries; others exalt them, perfect them in all sorts of ways, and even soon replace momentary losses by a visible increase in population, which is something quite extraordinary. History often shows us the spectacle of a rich and growing population in the midst of the most murderous battles. There are also vicious wars, accursed wars, that the conscience recognizes better than reasoning; nations are mortally wounded by them, both in their power and in their character; then you will see even the victor degraded, impoverished, and groaning under his sad laurels, whereas in lands of the vanquished, in a short time, you will not find an unused workshop or plough.

War is divine by the indefinable force that determines success in it. It was surely without thinking, my dear Chevalier, when you repeated the other day the celebrated maxim that *God is always on the side of the big battalions*. I will never believe that it really came from the great man to whom it has been attributed; perhaps he put forward this maxim in jest, or seriously in a limited and very true sense, for God in the temporal government of his Providence does not derogate, except in the case of miracles, from the general laws that he established for all time. Thus, just as two men are stronger than one, a hundred thousand men must be more powerful and effective than fifty thousand. When we ask God for victory, we do not ask him to derogate from the general laws of the world; that would be too much. However, these laws can combine in a thousand different ways, and can permit victory in ways that cannot be foreseen. Undoubtedly three men are stronger than one; this general proposition is incontestable, but an able man can profit from certain circumstances, and a single Horatius will kill three Curiatii. *A body with the greater mass has the greater momentum*; this is undoubtedly true if their speeds are equal, but three parts of mass and two of speed are equal to three parts of speed and two of mass. In the same way, an army of 40,000 men is physically inferior to another army of 60,000, but if the first has more courage, experience, and discipline, it will be able to defeat the second, for it is more effective with less mass. This is what we can see on every page of history. Moreover, war always supposes a certain equality between the two sides. I never read of the Republic of Ragusa declaring war on the sultans, or that of Geneva on the kings of France. There is always a certain equilibrium in the political world, and (if certain rare, precise, and limited cases are excepted) it is not up to man to upset it. This is why coalitions are so difficult. It they were not, since politics is so little governed by justice, coalitions would be assembled every day to destroy particular powers; but such projects seldom succeed, and history shows even weak powers escaping from them with astonishing ease. When a too predominate power frightens the world, men are irritated at not being able to find any way to check it, and bitter reproaches are made against the egotism and immorality of cabinets that are preventing an alliance against the common enemy. This is the cry that was heard in the heyday of Louis XIV. But in the end these complaints are ill founded. A coalition between several sovereigns,

Seventh Dialogue

based on a pure and disinterested morality, would be a miracle. God, who owes miracles to no one, and who never works them needlessly, uses two very simple means to re-establish political equilibrium: sometimes the giant overreaches itself, and sometimes a very inferior power puts a tiny obstacle in the giant's way, something imperceptible that subsequently grows in an unaccountable way until it becomes insurmountable, just as a small branch, stuck in the current of a river, can in the end produce a blockage that diverts it.

Starting, then, from this hypothesis of at least an approximate equilibrium, which is always the case, either because the two belligerent powers are equal or because the weakest has allies, how many unforeseen circumstances can upset the balance and can abort or promote the greatest projects despite all the calculations of human prudence! Four centuries before our era, geese saved the [Roman] Capitol; nine centuries into our era, under the Emperor Arnoulf, Rome was taken by a hare. I doubt whether the one or the other counted on such allies or feared such enemies. History is full of inconceivable events that disconcerted the finest speculations. Moreover, if you take a more general look at the role that moral power plays in war, you will be convinced that nowhere does the divine hand make itself felt more vividly to man. One could say that this is a *department*, if you will allow me the term, whose direction Providence has reserved to itself, and in which man is only allowed to act in an almost mechanical way, since success here depends almost entirely on what he can least control. Never is he warned more often and more vividly of his own powerlessness and of the inexorable power ruling all things than in war. *The intrepid Spartan used to sacrifice to fear* (Rousseau somewhere expressed astonishment at this, I don't know why); Alexander also sacrificed to fear before the Battle of Arbela. Certainly these people were quite right. To correct this sensible devotion, it suffices to pray to *God that he deigns not to send us fear*. Fear! Charles V made good fun of this epitaph that he read in passing: *Here lies one who never felt fear*. What man has never known fear in his life? Who has never had occasion to respect, both in himself, and in those around him and in history, the all-powerful weakness of this passion, which often seems to have more power over us the fewer the reasonable causes for it. *So let us pray*, Chevalier, *for it is to you, if you please, that this discourse is addressed*, since you have called forth these reflections. Let us pray to God with all our strength that he spares us and our friends from fear, which is within his power, and which, in an instant, can ruin the most splendid military plans.

Do not be frightened by this word *fear*, for if you take it in its strictest sense, you can say that what it expresses is rare, and that it is shameful to be afraid of it. There is a womanish fear that cries out in flight; and this sort we are permitted, even ordered, to regard as quite unacceptable, although it is not at all an unknown phenomenon. There is another much more terrible fear that descends into the most courageous heart, freezes it, and persuades it that it is defeated. This is the frightful scourge that always hangs over armies. One day I put this question to a first-class soldier whom you both know: *Tell me, General, what is a lost battle? This is something I have never understood.* After a moment's silence, he replied: *I just don't know.* Then, after another moment, he added: *It is a battle one believes one has lost.* Nothing is more true. One man fighting with another is defeated when he has been killed or brought to earth and the other remains standing. This is not the way it is with two armies; the one cannot be killed while the other remains on its feet. The forces swing back and forth as do the deaths, and especially since the invention of gunpowder has introduced more equality into the means of destruction, a battle is no longer lost materially, that is to say because there are more dead on one side than the other. It was Frederick II, who understood a little about these things, who said: *To win is to advance.* But who is the one who advances? It is the one whose conscience and countenance makes the other fall back. Do you recall, Count, that young soldier of your particular acquaintance who in one of his letters painted for you *that solemn moment when, without knowing why, an army senses itself advancing, as if it were sliding down an inclined plane.* I remember that you were struck by this phrase, which was a marvellous description of the crucial moment; but this moment is not at all a matter of reflection, nor is it, and this is particularly important to notice, in any way a question of numbers. Has the soldier *who slides forward* counted the dead? Opinion is so powerful in war that it can change the nature of the same event and even give it two different names, for no other reason than its own good pleasure. One general throws himself between two enemy armies, and writes to his court: *I have split him, he is lost.* The other writes to his court: *He has put himself between two fires, he is lost.* Which of the two is mistaken? The one who allows himself to be taken by the *cold goddess*. If all the circumstances, and the numbers especially, are at least approximately equal, show me a difference between the two sides that is not purely moral. The term *turn* is also one of those expressions that opinion *turns* in war, depending on how it is understood. Everyone knows the response the Spartan woman made to her son who complained of having too short a sword: *Step forward*. If the young man had been able to make himself heard on the battlefield and cried out to his mother: *I am turned*, the noble lady would not have failed to reply: *Turn the other*. It is imagination that loses battles.

It is not even by any means always on the day that they take place that it is known whether they have been won or lost; it is on the next day, or often two or three days afterward. People talk a lot about battles without knowing what they are really like. In particular, they tend to consider them as occurring at one place, whereas they cover two or three leagues of country. They ask you seriously: *How is it that you don't know what happened in this battle, since you were there?* Whereas it is precisely the opposite that would often have to be said. Does the one on the right know what is happening on the left? Does he even know what is happening two paces from him?

I can easily imagine one of these frightful scenes. On a vast field covered with all the apparatus of carnage and seeming to shudder under the feet of men and horses, in the midst of fire and whirling smoke, dazed and carried away by the din of firearms and cannon, by voices that

Seventh Dialogue

order, roar, and die away, surrounded by the dead, the dying, and mutilated corpses, seized in turn by fear, hope, and rage, by five or six different passions, what happens to a man? What does he see? What does he know after a few hours? What can he know about himself and others? Among this crowd of warriors who have fought the whole day, there is often not a single one, not even the general, who knows who the victor is. I will restrict myself to citing modern battles, famous battles whose memory will never perish, battles that have changed the face of Europe and that were only lost because such and such a man thought they were lost; they were battles where all circumstances being equal and without a drop of more blood being shed on either side, the other general could have had a *Te Deum* sung in his own country and forced history to record the opposite of what it will say. Yet, for heaven's sake, what period has ever seen moral power play a more astonishing role in war than our own times? Is there not real magic in what we have seen the last twenty years? Undoubtedly men of this epoch can cry out: *And what age has been more fertile in miracles?*

Without leaving the topic that now occupies us, has there been in this genre a single event contrary to the most obvious calculations of probability that we have not seen occur despite all the efforts of human prudence? Have we not even seen won battles lost? In any case, gentlemen, I don't want to exaggerate anything, for you know that I have a particular hatred of exaggeration, which is the falsehood of honest men. For the little that you find of exaggeration in what I have just said, I pass sentence without dispute, so much the more willingly in that I have no need to be correct in the fullest sense of the term. In general, I believe that battles are not won or lost physically. There is nothing rigid about this proposition, which can be subject to all the restrictions you judge convenient, provided that in your turn you agree with me (and this is something that no man can deny) that moral power has an immense effect in war, which is all that I need. So let us no longer speak of *big battalions*, Chevalier, for no idea, if we restrict it in the sense that I have just explained, is more deceptive and crude.

The Count

Your country, Senator, was not saved by *big battalions*, when at the beginning of the seventeenth century Prince Pozharsky and a horse merchant named Minin delivered it from an insupportable yoke. The honest merchant promised his goods and those of his friends in assisting Pozharsky, who promised his arms and his blood; they began with a thousand men, and they succeeded.

The Senator

I am charmed that your memory recalls this episode, but the history of every nation is filled with similar facts demonstrating how the power of numbers can be produced, enhanced, weakened, or nullified by a host of circumstances beyond our control. As for our *Te Deums*,

Seventh Dialogue

so frequent and so often misplaced, I willingly abandon them to you, Chevalier. If God resembled us, they would attract his anger, but he knows what we are and treats us according to our ignorance. In any case, although there are abuses in this matter as in all things human, the general custom is no less sound and praiseworthy.

We must always ask God for success and always thank him for it, since nothing in the world is more immediately dependent on God than war. Since here he restricts man's natural power, and since he loves to be called *the God of war*, there are all sorts of reasons for us to redouble our entreaties when we are struck by this terrible scourge. Christian nations have still more reason to be in tacit agreement, when their armies succeed, in expressing their thankfulness to *the God of hosts* by a *Te Deum*, for I do not think it would be possible to employ a more beautiful prayer to thank him for the victories that he gives. We owe this prayer to your church, Count.

The Count

Yes, it was born in Italy, from all appearances, and the title *Ambrosian hymn* would lead us to believe that it was exclusively the work of St Ambrose. However, it is commonly enough believed, simply on the basis of tradition to be sure, that the *Te Deum* was *improvised*, if we may use that term, in a transport of religious fervour in Milan by the two great and holy doctors St Ambrose and St Augustine, an opinion that appears very probable. In fact, this inimitable canticle, preserved and translated by your church and by Protestant communions, presents not the least trace of labour and reflection. It is not a *composition*, it is an *effusion*; it is burning poetry, free of all metre, it is a divine dithyramb where enthusiasm, flying on its own wings, scorns all the resources of art. I doubt whether faith, love, and thanksgiving have ever spoken a truer and more penetrating language.

The Chevalier

I remember what you said in our last dialogue about the intrinsic character of different prayers. This is a subject I have never thought about, but you have made me eager to take *a course on prayers*. This will be a topic of erudition, for all nations have prayed.

The Count

This will be a very interesting course and it will not be pure erudition. Along the way you will find a host of interesting observations, for each nation's prayer is a kind of indicator that shows us with mathematical precision the nation's moral standing. The Hebrews, for example, sometimes gave God the name *father*; even the pagans made great use of this title. However, when it comes to prayer, it is something else; you will not find in all of pagan antiquity, nor even in the Old Testament, a single example of man giving God the title *father* in speaking to him in prayer. Again, why is it that, apart

Seventh Dialogue

from the revelation of Moses, none in antiquity knew how to express repentance in their prayers? Like us, they knew remorse, since they had a conscience; their great criminals traversed earth and sea to find expiation and victims. They incensed themselves, they immersed themselves in water and blood, but they never experienced a *contrite heart*; they never knew how to ask pardon in their prayers. Ovid, like a thousand others, could put these words in the mouth of the outraged man who pardoned the criminal: *non quia tu dignus, sed quia mitis ego* [not that you merit it but that I need it], but no one in antiquity could put these words in the mouth of a criminal talking to God. We seem to translate Ovid in the liturgy of the Mass when we say: *Non æstimator meriti, sed veniæ largitor admitte* [Not according to our merits but according to thy great mercy]; and yet we are then saying what the entire human race could never learn to say without revelation, for men knew well that they could *irritate* God or *a god*, but not that they could *offend him*. The words *crime* and *criminal* are found in all languages, but *sin* and *sinner* belong to Christian language. For a similar reason, men have always called God *father*, which expresses a relationship of creation and power, but no man on his own could say *my father*, since this is a relationship of love foreign even to Mount Sinai, and which belongs only to Calvary.

One more observation: the barbarism of the Hebrew people is one of the favourite theses of the eighteenth century: it is not permitted to acknowledge that this people possessed any science whatsoever; they did not know the least truth in physics and astronomy; for them the earth was only a *flat plate*, the heavens only a *canopy*; its language was derived from another, and none derived from it; they never achieved either philosophy, arts, or literature; never until a very late date did foreign nations have the least knowledge of the books of Moses, and it is very false to think that superior truths disseminated in the writers of pagan antiquity came from that source. Let us obligingly agree to all this; how is it then that this nation was constantly sensible, interesting, touching, and very often even sublime and delightful in its prayers? In general, the Bible includes a host of prayers from which we have made a book in our own language; but it includes, moreover, the book of books in this genre, the book par excellence, the one without rival, the Book of Psalms.

The Senator

We have already had a long conversation with the Chevalier on the Book of Psalms; on this subject I complained to him, as I complain to yourself, about not understanding Slavonic, for the translation of the Psalms that we possess in this language is a masterpiece.

The Count

I don't doubt it; everyone agrees on this, and besides your opinion suffices for me. However, on this point you must forgive my prejudices and unalterable views.

Seventh Dialogue

Three languages were consecrated on Calvary: Hebrew, Greek, and Latin. I would like to stick with them; two languages for private prayer, one for church – that is enough. For the rest, I honour all the efforts that have been made in this respect in all nations; but you know well that we are scarcely likely to agree.

The Chevalier

I repeat to you what I said the other day to our dear Senator when talking about the same subject: I admire David a bit as I admire Pindar, on hearsay.

The Count

What are you saying, my dear Chevalier? Pindar has nothing in common with David. The first has himself taken care to inform us *that he spoke only to the learned, and that he cared little about being understood by the mass of his contemporaries, for whom he would not be upset to require interpreters*. To understand this poet perfectly it is not enough to *pronounce* him or even to *sing* him; he must be *danced*. Someday I will tell you about this quite astonishing new *Dorian measure* that is prescribed by Pindar's impetuous muse. However, when you have come to understand him as perfectly as one can in our times, you will be little interested. Pindar's odes are the kind of corpses from which the spirit has retired forever. What do the *horses of Hièron* or the *mules of Agèsias* matter to you? What interest do you have in the nobility of his cities or their founders, in the miracles of the gods, the exploits of his heroes, or the love affairs of his nymphs? His charm belonged to certain times and places; no effort of the imagination can bring them to life again for us. There is no more Olympus, no more Elis, no more Alpheus; someone who thought they could find the Peloponnesus in Peru would be less ridiculous than the one who looked for it in the Morea.

David, on the other hand, defies time and place because he accorded nothing to place and circumstance; he sang only of God and his immortal truths. Jerusalem has not disappeared for us: *it is everywhere we are*; and it is David especially who makes it present to us. Therefore read the Psalms and read them unceasingly; not, if you take my advice, in our modern translations, which are too far from the source, but in the Latin version adopted in our church. I know that Hebraisms, always somewhat visible through the Vulgate, can be astonishing at first glance, for the Psalms as we read them today, although not translated directly from the original, are nevertheless derived from a version that was itself very close to the Hebrew, so that the difficulty is the same. However, this difficulty quickly gives way to an honest effort. *Choose a friend who*, without knowing Hebrew, can nevertheless by attentive and repeated reading penetrate the spirit of a language that is incomparably more ancient than any other whose remnants survive. It is a language whose logical laconism is more cumbersome for us than the most hardy grammatical brevity, and which accustoms us especially to grasping the almost invisible Oriental

Seventh Dialogue

link between ideas, a bounding genius that understands nothing of European nuances. You will see that the essential merit of the Vulgate translation is to have known how to be both close enough and far enough from the Hebrew; you will see how a syllable, a word, how some indescribable assistance lightly given to a phrase, brings forth first-order beauties before our eyes. The Psalms are a veritable *gospel preparation*, for nowhere is the spirit of prayer, which is that of God, more visible, and everywhere we read there the promises of all that we possess. The primary characteristic of these hymns is that they always pray. Even when the subject of a Psalm appears accidental and quite relative to some event in the life of the prophet-king, his genius always escapes this limited circle. He always generalizes since he sees everything within the immense unity of the power that inspires him; he turns all his thoughts and all his feelings into prayers. There is not a line that does not belong to all ages and to all men. He never needs that indulgence that permits enthusiasm to be obscure, and yet nevertheless when the eagle of Cedron takes its flight towards the clouds, your eye will be able to measure beneath him *more air* than Horace once saw under the swan of Dirce. Sometimes he allows himself to be penetrated by the idea of the presence of God, and the most magnificent expressions crowd his mind:

> Where can I hide from your spirit?
> And where can I flee from your face?
> If I take the wings of the dawn,
> if I dwell in the uttermost part of the sea:

> even there will your hand guide me,
> and your right hand hold me.
> If I ascend into heaven, you are there;
> if I lie down with the dead, you are there.

Sometimes his eyes turn towards nature, and his rapture teaches us how we must envision it:

> For you delight me, O Lord, by your deeds,
> I rejoice in the works of your hands.
> How great are your works, O Lord,
> how deep your thoughts!
> The senseless man knows not,
> nor does the fool understand these things.

If he descends to particular phenomena, what an abundance of images! You see with what vigour and grace he expresses the *wedding* of the earth and its watering:

> You have visited the earth and watered it,
> greatly have you enriched it.
> The river of God abounds with water,
> You have prepared grain for them;
> for thus have you prepared it.
> Its furrows you have prepared,
> its clods you have made smooth,
> with showers you have softened it,
> You have blessed its sprouting seed.
> You have crowned the year with your kindness,
> your clouds will distil abundance.
> The pasture lands of the desert drip,

Seventh Dialogue

> and the hills gird themselves with great joy.
> The fields are clothed with your flocks,
> and the valleys are covered with grain:
> they cry aloud and sing.

It is in the loftiest realms that he must be heard to explain the marvels of this interior worship that in his time could only have been perceived by inspiration. The divine love that embraces him lends him a prophetic character; he anticipates the centuries and he already belongs to the law of grace. Like Francis de Sales or Fénelon, he discovers in the human heart *these mysterious decrees that lead us from strength to strength until we shall see the God of gods*. He is inexhaustible when he exalts the sweetness and excellence of the divine law.

> [This law] is a lantern for his uncertain feet,
> a light, a star, that light for him the dark paths of life.
> It is truth, it is truth itself,
> it carries its justification within itself;
> it is sweeter than honey,
> more desirable than gold and precious stones;
> and those who are loyal to it,
> find there unlimited recompense.
> He meditates on it day and night.
> He treasures God's oracles in his heart
> so that he may not offend against Him.
> If you will give me a docile heart,
> I will run in the way of your commands.

Sometimes the feeling that oppresses him stops his breath. A word coming forth to express the prophet's thought halts on his lips and falls back to his heart; but piety will understand him when he cries out: YOUR ALTARS, O LORD OF HOSTS!

Other times we hear him foreshadowing all of Christianity in a few words. *Teach me*, he says, *to do your will, because you are my God.* What philosopher of antiquity ever knew that virtue is nothing but obedience to God *because he is God*, and that merit depends exclusively on this obedient conduct of thought?

He knew well the terrible law of our defiled nature; he knew that men *are conceived in inequity, and rebel against the divine law from their mother's womb.* As well as the great apostle he knew that *man is a slave sold to the iniquity that has him under its yoke, so that only where the Spirit of the Lord is, is there freedom.* Thus he cried out with a truly Christian exactness: *Through you I am snatched from temptation, with your assistance I leap the wall.* This wall of separation raised from the beginning between man and the Creator, this wall absolutely must *be cleared*, since it cannot be *overturned*, and when he says to God *Give me a sign*, does he not confess, does he not teach the whole truth? On the one side, *nothing in us*, and on the other, *nothing without you*. If man boldly dares to rely on himself, vengeance is all ready: *He is delivered up to the inclinations of his heart and to the dreams of his imagination.*

Certain that man of himself is incapable of prayer, David asks God to fill him *with this mysterious oil, with this divine unction that will open his lips and allow them to pronounce words of praise and elation.* Since he only tells

Seventh Dialogue

us his own experience, he lets us see the work of inspiration in him. *I felt my heart grow hot within me*, he says, *a fire blazed forth from my thoughts. Then my tongue was freed and I spoke.* Compare these chaste flames of divine love, these sublime outbursts of a spirit delighted with heaven to the putrid heat of Sappho or the paid enthusiasm of Pindar. Taste alone can decide, virtue is not required.

See how the prophet deciphered the unbeliever with a single phrase: *He refused to believe, for fear of acting rightly*, and how, again in a single phrase, he gives a terrible lesson to believers when he tells them: *You who profess to love God must therefore hate evil.*

This extraordinary man, enriched with such precious gifts, nevertheless made himself enormously guilty; but atonement enriched his hymns with new beauties. Never has the repentant sinner spoken a truer, more pathetic, more penetrating language. *Ready to receive all the scourges of the Lord with resignation, he is ready to admit his iniquities. His sin is ever before his eyes, and his grief is with him always.* In the middle of Jerusalem, in the heart of that sumptuous capital soon destined to become *by far the most famous city in the East*, on the throne where he had been led by the hand of God, *he is like the pelican of the desert, like an owl among the ruins, like a bird all alone on the housetop. He has wearied himself with groaning, night after night he waters his couch with his weeping. The arrows of the Lord have pierced him. For there is nothing healthy in him, his bones are broken, There is no health in his flesh; he is stooped and bowed down profoundly; all the day he goes in mourning: he no longer hears; he has lost his voice; all that remains to him is hope*. Nothing can distract him from his sorrow, and this sorrow always turning him towards prayer like all his other feelings, his prayer has something living that can be found nowhere else. He unceasingly recalls the oracle he has pronounced against himself: *God says to the sinner: 'Why do you declare my precepts with your impure mouth?' I want praise only from the virtuous*. So with the psalmist, terror is always mixed with confidence, and even in the transports of love, in the ecstasy of admiration, in the most touching effusions of unlimited thanksgiving, the sharp point of remorse makes itself felt like the thorn in a ruby bunch of roses.

Finally, nothing strikes me more forcefully in these magnificent psalms than the breadth of the prophet's religious ideas; although restricted to a small point on the globe, the ideas he professed are nevertheless distinguished by a marked leaning towards universality. The temple in Jerusalem was open to all nations, and the disciple of Moses did not refuse to pray to his God with any man or for any man; full of these great and generous ideas, and, moreover, pushed by a prophetic spirit that showed him in advance *the swiftness of his word and the power of his good news*, David never ceased to address the human race and to call all mankind to the truth. This call to the light, this heartfelt pledge, is always present in his sublime compositions. To express this in a thousand ways, he exhausted the language without ever being able to satisfy himself. *Hear this, all you nations; give ear, all you inhabitants of time. The Lord is good to all, and merciful to all his works. Your kingdom is a kingdom of all ages, and endures through all ages. Shout with joy all you lands. Let all*

Seventh Dialogue

the earth adore you and sing to you, let it sing your name. Bless our God, O nations, and declare the fame of his praise. Say to God: How tremendous are your deeds, for your great strength your enemies fawn upon you. Let kings of the earth and all the nations, let princes and judges of the earth, let them praise the name of the Lord because his name alone is exalted. I am the friend of all who fear you and keep your commandments. Kings, princes, the great and all peoples who cover the earth praise the name of the Lord, for his name only is great. Then the peoples gather, and the kingdoms, to serve the Lord. Nations of the earth, applaud and sing, sing to your king! Sing, for your Lord is king of the world. SING WITH INTELLIGENCE. *Let everything that has breath praise the Lord!*

God did not disdain to satisfy this great desire. The prophetic view of the holy king, in burying itself in the far future, already saw the great explosion of the *cenacle* and the face of the earth renewed by the effusion of the divine spirit. How beautiful are his expressions, and especially how appropriate! *All the ends of the earth* SHALL REMEMBER *and shall be converted to the Lord; and all the families of the nations shall bow down in his sight.*

Wise friends, let us notice here in passing how infinite goodness could *overlook forty centuries*; it awaited the *remembrance* of man. I will finish by recalling for you another wish of the prophet-king: *Let these things be written for a generation to come, and let a people that shall be created, praise the Lord.*

His wish was fulfilled. Because he sang only of the Eternal, his hymns participated in eternity. The fiery accents imparted to his divine lyre still resound in all parts of the world after thirty centuries. The synagogue preserved the Psalms; the Church hastened to adopt them. The poetry of all Christian nations has laid hold of them, and for more than three centuries the sun has never ceased to shine on churches whose vaults resound to these sacred hymns. They are sung in Rome, Geneva, Madrid, London, Quebec, Quito, Moscow, Peking, and Botany Bay; they are whispered in Japan.

The Chevalier

Can you tell me why I cannot recall having read in the Psalms anything of what you have just told me?

The Count

Of course, my young friend, *I can tell you why*. This phenomenon belongs to the theory of innate ideas. Although there are original notions common to all men, without which they would not be men, and which are in consequence accessible, or rather natural, to all minds, it is nevertheless unnecessary for all minds to arrive at the same point. On the contrary, some ideas are somewhat dormant and others are more or less dominant in each mind; and this forms what is called its *character* or its *talent*. So it happens that when we receive some sort of spiritual food through reading, each mind appropriates to itself what particularly suits what I would call its *intellectual temperament*, and the rest escapes it. This is why we do not all read the same things when we read the same books; which is what happens especially with the other sex compared to our own, for women do not read as we do. This difference being so general, and at the same time so obvious, I invite you to reflect on it.

The Senator

The night that is catching up with us recalls for me, Count, since you are carrying on so well, that you could very well have recalled for us something that David said about the night. This is something that concerned him very much and that he talked about a great deal, and I have been expecting among all the outstanding texts that have struck you some on the night, for this is a great subject to which David often returned; and who could be surprised by this. You know very well, my good friends, that the night is dangerous for man, and that without perceiving it we all love it a little because it puts us at ease. Night is the natural accomplice constantly at the service of every vice, and this seductive indulgence means that we generally value the night much less than the day. Light intimidates vice; darkness lends it all its forces, and this is what virtue fears. Again, night is of no value for man, and, yet, and perhaps even because of this, are we not all a little idolatrous of this easy divinity? Who can pride himself on never having invoked it for evil? From the highway brigand to the salon wrongdoer, what man has never said: *Flecte, precor vultus ad mea furta tuos* [Turn, I beg, your face to my thefts]? Again, what man has never said: *Nox conscia novit* [The night shares your secret and knows]? The best society, the best regulated family, is the one that stays up the least; and the extreme corruption of morals always announces its presence by the extremity of abuses of this kind. Night being, therefore, by its nature, *malè suada* [a persuader of evil], a bad counsellor, it follows that false religions have often consecrated their criminal rites to it, *nota bonæ secreta deæ* [well known for all the mysteries of the good Goddess].

The Count

With your permission, my dear friend, I would rather say that *antique corruption* consecrated the night to criminal orgies, but that *antique religion* was not wrong, or was less wrong than impotent, for I believe that nothing begins with evil. For example, antique religion put these mysteries that you have just mentioned under the care of the most severe modesty; it chased even the smallest male animal from the temple – even paintings of men; the poet whom you have just cited himself recalls this law with his mad gaiety in order to make a frightening contrast stand out better. You see that the original intentions could not have been clearer; I would add that even in the bosom of error the nocturnal prayer of the Vestal seems to have been invented to provide a balance at some point to the mysteries of the good goddess; but the true cult must have distinguished itself on this point and lacked nothing. If night gives bad counsel, as you have just said, it must also be rendered justice for it

Seventh Dialogue

also gives excellent counsel. It is a time of profound meditations and sublime delights; in order to profit from these divine effusions and in order also to counteract the deadly influence of which you spoke, Christianity in its turn has also seized the night and consecrated to it holy ceremonies that it animates with austere music and powerful canticles. Even religion, in everything that does not pertain to dogma, is subject to certain changes that our poor nature make inevitable; nevertheless down to matters of pure discipline certain things are always invariable. For example, there will always be feast-days that will call us all to the night office, and *always* there will be chosen men whose pious voices will be heard in the darkness, since legitimate praise must never be silent on the earth:

> The day recalls it to the day,
> And the night announces it to the night.

The Senator

Alas! Who knows if you are not expressing a wish rather than a truth, at least at the moment! How the reign of prayer has been weakened, and what means have not been used to extinguish its voice! Has our century not asked *Of what use are those who pray?* How can prayer pierce the darkness, when it is scarcely allowed to make itself heard by day? However, I don't want to go astray in these sad forebodings. You have said everything I wanted to say about the night, without however saying what David said of it, and this is what I wanted you to supply. In my turn I now ask for your permission to proceed with my principle idea. Full of ideas he owed to no man, David never ceased exhorting man *to suspend his sleep to pray*; he thought that the august silence of the night lent a particular strength to holy desires. *I sought God in the night*, he said, *and I was not deceived*. Elsewhere he says: *During the night I meditate within my heart, I think back, and my spirit searches diligently*. In musing another time on certain dangers that must have been stronger in antiquity than in our time, he said in his victorious conscience: *O Lord, I remember your name in the night, and I will keep your law*. Undoubtedly he believed that the influence of the night was the test of hearts, since he added: *You tested my heart, searching it in the night*.

Night air is worthless for the material man; animals teach us this since they all stop their activities to sleep. Our illnesses teach us this by dealing most severely with all of us at night. Why do you inquire in the morning of your friend to ask *how he passed the night*, rather than asking in the evening *how he has passed the day*? It must be because there is something bad about the night. From this comes the necessity of sleep, which is not made for the day, and which is no less necessary for the mind as for the body, for they are both continually exposed to the action of certain powers that unceasingly attack them so that neither could *live*; so it is necessary that these harmful actions are periodically suspended and that they are both put under a protective influence during these intervals. Just as the body continues its vital functions

Seventh Dialogue

during sleep, without the sensible principle being conscious of it, the *vital* functions of the mind continue as well, as you can convince yourself independently of all theory by a common experience, since man can learn during sleep, and know, for example, on waking, verses, or the tune of a song that he did not know on going to sleep.

However, for the analogy to be perfect, the intelligent principle must not even be conscious of what happened to it during this time, or at least that it have no memory of it, which amounts to the same thing with respect to the established order. From the universal belief that man then finds himself under a good and preserving influence, comes another belief, likewise universal, *that the time of sleep is favourable to divine communications*. This opinion, in whatever way it might be understood, is incontestably based on Holy Scripture, which presents a great number of cases of this kind. Moreover we see that false religions have always professed the same belief, for error, in turning its back on its rival nevertheless never ceases to repeat all its acts and all its doctrines, which it alters according to its character, that is to say in such a way that the model can never be misidentified nor the image taken for the reality. Middleton and other writers of the same sort have used great erudition to prove that your church *imitates* a host of pagan ceremonies, a reproach that they would also address to ours if they ever thought of us. Deceived by a negative religion and by a fleshless cult, they misunderstood the eternal forms of a positive religion that can be found everywhere. In America, modern travellers have found Vestals, new fire, circumcision, baptism, confession, and finally the *real presence*, under the *species* of *bread* and *wine*.

Do we say that we owe these ceremonies to the Mexicans or the Peruvians? We must always take care not to conclude from conformity to subordinate derivation; for the reasoning to be legitimate, common derivation must have been previously excluded. Moreover, to return to the night and to dreams, we see that the greatest geniuses of antiquity, without distinction, never doubted the importance of dreams, and that they even went so far as to sleep in temples to receive oracles there. Did not Job say that *God uses dreams to warn men*, AND REPEATETH NOT THE SELFSAME THING A SECOND TIME, and did not David say, as I recalled for you a little while ago, *that God visits hearts in the night*? Did Plato not want us *to prepare for dreams by great purity of soul and body*? Did not Hippocrates compose a special treatise on dreams, where he went so far as to refuse to accept as a real doctor anyone who could not interpret dreams? It seems to me that a Latin poet, Lucretius if I am not mistaken, went even farther in saying *that during sleep the gods speak to the soul and to the mind*.

Finally, Marcus Aurelius (I do not cite a weak mind here) not only regarded these nocturnal communications as an incontestable fact, but he declared moreover, in his own terms, of having received them. What do you say to that, gentlemen? Would you by chance want to maintain that all the sacred and profane science of antiquity talked nonsense? That men have never seen what they have seen, experienced what they have experi-

Seventh Dialogue

enced? That the great men I have cited for you had weak minds? That . . .

The Chevalier

For myself, I do not believe that I have yet acquired the right to be impertinent.

The Senator

As for me, I also believe that no one has the right to acquire this right, which, thanks to God, does not exist.

The Count

Tell me, my dear friend, why you would not collect a host of the very elevated and quite uncommon thoughts that constantly come to you when we are talking of metaphysics or religion? You could entitle this collection *Philosophic Flights*. If fact, there exists a work with the same title written in Latin; *but these are flights that could break your neck*; yours, it seems to me, could uplift man without danger.

Joseph de Maistre

The Chevalier

I also exhort you to do this, my dear Senator. While waiting, gentlemen, something will happen to me, thanks to you, that certainly never happened before in my life: this is to go to sleep thinking of *the prophet king*. To your honour!

1. Seneca *On the Shortness of Life*
2. Marcus Aurelius *Meditations*
3. St Augustine *Confessions of a Sinner*
4. Thomas à Kempis *The Inner Life*
5. Niccolò Machiavelli *The Prince*
6. Michel de Montaigne *On Friendship*
7. Jonathan Swift *A Tale of a Tub*
8. Jean-Jacques Rousseau *The Social Contract*
9. Edward Gibbon *The Christians and the Fall of Rome*
10. Thomas Paine *Common Sense*
11. Mary Wollstonecraft *A Vindication of the Rights of Woman*
12. William Hazlitt *On the Pleasure of Hating*
13. Karl Marx & Friedrich Engels *The Communist Manifesto*
14. Arthur Schopenhauer *On the Suffering of the World*
15. John Ruskin *On Art and Life*
16. Charles Darwin *On Natural Selection*
17. Friedrich Nietzsche *Why I am So Wise*
18. Virginia Woolf *A Room of One's Own*
19. Sigmund Freud *Civilization and Its Discontents*
20. George Orwell *Why I Write*

21. Confucius *The First Ten Books*
22. Sun-tzu *The Art of War*
23. Plato *The Symposium*
24. Lucretius *Sensation and Sex*
25. Cicero *An Attack on an Enemy of Freedom*
26. *The Revelation of St John the Divine* and *The Book of Job*
27. Marco Polo *Travels in the Land of Kubilai Khan*
28. Christine de Pizan *The City of Ladies*
29. Baldesar Castiglione *How to Achieve True Greatness*
30. Francis Bacon *Of Empire*
31. Thomas Hobbes *Of Man*
32. Sir Thomas Browne *Urne-Burial*
33. Voltaire *Miracles and Idolatry*
34. David Hume *On Suicide*
35. Carl von Clausewitz *On the Nature of War*
36. Søren Kierkegaard *Fear and Trembling*
37. Henry David Thoreau *Where I Lived, and What I Lived For*
38. Thorstein Veblen *Conspicuous Consumption*
39. Albert Camus *The Myth of Sisyphus*
40. Hannah Arendt *Eichmann and the Holocaust*

41. Plutarch *In Consolation to his Wife*
42. Robert Burton *Some Anatomies of Melancholy*
43. Blaise Pascal *Human Happiness*
44. Adam Smith *The Invisible Hand*
45. Edmund Burke *The Evils of Revolution*
46. Ralph Waldo Emerson *Nature*
47. Søren Kierkegaard *The Sickness unto Death*
48. John Ruskin *The Lamp of Memory*
49. Friedrich Nietzsche *Man Alone with Himself*
50. Leo Tolstoy *A Confession*
51. William Morris *Useful Work v. Useless Toil*
52. Frederick Jackson Turner *The Significance of the Frontier in American History*
53. Marcel Proust *Days of Reading*
54. Leon Trotsky *An Appeal to the Toiling, Oppressed and Exhausted Peoples of Europe*
55. Sigmund Freud *The Future of an Illusion*
56. Walter Benjamin *The Work of Art in the Age of Mechanical Reproduction*
57. George Orwell *Books v. Cigarettes*
58. Albert Camus *The Fastidious Assassins*
59. Frantz Fanon *Concerning Violence*
60. Michel Foucault *The Spectacle of the Scaffold*

61. Lao Tzu *Tao Te Ching*
62. *Writings from the Zen Masters*
63. Thomas More *Utopia*
64. Michel de Montaigne *On Solitude*
65. William Shakespeare *On Power*
66. John Locke *Of the Abuse of Words*
67. Samuel Johnson *Consolation in the Face of Death*
68. Immanuel Kant *An Answer to the Question: 'What is Enlightenment?'*
69. Joseph de Maistre *The Executioner*
70. Thomas De Quincey *Confessions of an English Opium Eater*
71. Arthur Schopenhauer *The Horrors and Absurdities of Religion*
72. Abraham Lincoln *The Gettysburg Address*
73. Karl Marx *Revolution and War*
74. Fyodor Dostoyevsky *The Grand Inquisitor*
75. William James *On a Certain Blindness in Human Beings*
76. Robert Louis Stevenson *An Apology for Idlers*
77. W. E. B. Du Bois *Of the Dawn of Freedom*
78. Virginia Woolf *Thoughts on Peace in an Air Raid*
79. George Orwell *Decline of the English Murder*
80. John Berger *Why Look at Animals?*

THE STORY OF PENGUIN CLASSICS

Before 1946 ...'Classics' are mainly the domain of academics and students, without readable editions for everyone else. This all changes when a little-known classicist, E. V. Rieu, presents Penguin founder Allen Lane with the translation of Homer's Odyssey that he has been working on and reading to his wife Nelly in his spare time.

1946 The Odyssey becomes the first Penguin Classic published, and promptly sells three million copies. Suddenly, classic books are no longer for the privileged few.

1950s Rieu, now series editor, turns to professional writers for the best modern, readable translations, including Dorothy L. Sayers's *Inferno* and Robert Graves's *The Twelve Caesars*, which revives the salacious original.

1960s 1961 sees the arrival of the Penguin Modern Classics, showcasing the best twentieth-century writers from around the world. Rieu retires in 1964, hailing the Penguin Classics list as 'the greatest educative force of the 20th century'.

1970s A new generation of translators arrives to swell the Penguin Classics ranks, and the list grows to encompass more philosophy, religion, science, history and politics.

1980s The Penguin American Library joins the Classics stable, with titles such as *The Last of the Mohicans* safeguarded. Penguin Classics now offers the most comprehensive library of world literature available.

1990s Penguin Popular Classics are launched, offering readers budget editions of the greatest works of literature. Penguin Audiobooks brings the classics to a listening audience for the first time, and in 1999 the launch of the Penguin Classics website takes them online to an ever larger global readership.

The 21st Century Penguin Classics are rejacketed for the first time in nearly twenty years. This world famous series now consists of more than 1,300 titles, making the widest range of the best books ever written available to millions – and constantly redefining the meaning of what makes a 'classic'.

The Odyssey continues ...

The best books ever written

PENGUIN CLASSICS

SINCE 1946

Find out more at www.penguinclassics.com